PLATE I. *SPRING LYRIC*

*Perfect rhythm in line and in color, and a subtle suggestion of dancing
motion are incorporated in this "picture," which also illustrates well the
new trend of making the accessories an integral part of the composition.*

Mrs. Dexter M. Ferry, Jr., Garden Club of Michigan
International Flower Show, New York
Class: Flower picture.   No restrictions, except proportion to
    space; 1st prize.

Flower Arrangement in Color

By

F. F. ROCKWELL *and* E. C. GRAYSON

With an Introduction by

MRS. FREDERICK A. WALLIS

Color Photography by

FREDRICK W. CASSEBEER

WISE & CO., INC.

New York

Foreword

$\mathcal{F}$ OR MANY YEARS it has seemed to me a matter of the greatest regret that the beauty in flower arrangements so painstakingly and perfectly wrought should, almost in the moment of its achievement, perish forever from the earth. A compelling desire to try in some way to preserve that beauty, at least in part, for the future enjoyment and inspiration of others was the genesis of this book.

The obstacles in the way of accomplishing this result seemed at first insurmountable. Black and white photographs, even good ones, render but the skeleton of a flower arrangement. In addition to the expense involved in procuring natural color photographs, there loomed up the physical obstacles of taking them under the almost impossible conditions existing at most flower shows. And beyond that there was the still more staggering problem of the cost of the color plates.

Thanks to the cooperation of a number of good friends, FLOWER ARRANGEMENT IN COLOR is at last an accomplished fact.

The book, of course, will not satisfy everyone. Some critics will think that many of the arrangements shown are too amateurish, or not—in the expert's use of the term—"arrangements" at all; others will feel, on the contrary, that too many of them are flower show pieces, more complicated or elaborate then the average flower lover could attempt in her own home.

To the former may I point out that this volume is not meant only for the advanced student of the art of arrangement, but for all who love and grow flowers—including the busy working gardener who must depend upon her own garden as a source of material, and who can spare but little time in arranging it. And to those who feel that too high a standard has been set, let me add that there is no suggestion that they try to imitate, but that the study—or even the repeated observation—of excellent arrangements will enable them to obtain more satisfying results in their own use of flowers, no matter on how simple a scale they may work.

So if this volume has helped to rescue from complete oblivion even a few of the masterpieces in this new—but unfortunately so ephemeral— art; and if it serves as an inspiration to those who, either as serious students or rank amateurs, wish to make the flowers they use more effective as decoration, it will have served its purpose.

And in closing this foreword the authors wish to take the opportunity to acknowledge the generous assistance that has made the present volume possible. The cordial co-operation of the Federated Garden Clubs of New York and the Garden Club of New Jersey, and many members of the Garden Club of America have made available many of the photographs reproduced.

The assistance, particularly, of Mrs. Robert Kearfott and Mrs. Grace Lincoln, both of whom have been outstanding leaders in the development of American flower art, who have been especially generous in helping to select the subjects for reproduction, in suggestions and criticisms, and in the preparation of the comments on the subjects reproduced in color, is appreciated. To my friend,

Mr. Faber Birren, whose research and published works in the difficult realm of color have won world-wide recognition, I am indebted for the privilege of reproducing the color chart on page *89* and for valuable suggestions in connection with the discussion of color. And thanks are also due to Miss Margaret Sorensen for the drawings which appear in the book.

F. F. R.

Table of Contents

TABLE OF CONTENTS

[xi]

List of Color Plates

LIST OF COLOR PLATES

LIST OF COLOR PLATES

Introduction

*I*N SPITE of the criticism and fun often thrust at the wildly enthusiastic who go in for "Flower Arrangements" so ardently, it is an established fact, nevertheless, that this art has never been more popular than to-day. Wherever there are sections in flower shows given over to this particular art, there you will find visitors in great numbers enchanted by the exhibits, and literally in ecstasies over the beauty assembled in artistic arrangements from the leaf and flowering world.

We are deeply grateful to the authors for preserving for our generation, and for generations to come, the natural beauty and grace and color, that have glorified the great flower shows of our country. I believe I shall never cease to wonder at this marvelous miracle of photography. Perfect colors reproduced in pictures is one of the startling and delightful surprises which science has given our age.

These pictures have been selected with utmost care and much study and cover a wide range of composition. In some of the arrangements you will sense a pleasing atmosphere, or a charm of detail workmanship that is captivating. In another arrangement a sort of mystery that is indescribable. In still another an absolute perfection of design, and in others just the true beauty of the flowers may appeal. The whole presentation is a beautiful study commanding our admiration.

In flowers and in plant material there is an indescribably lovesome quality which they possess in their own right—the creation of God and not of man. To work with such materials gives to the artist a larger field of exploration, more fascinating than tubes of paint or brush could ever offer. The brilliancy and perfect blending of colors in harmony, the exquisite delicacy of some blossoms, and the form, light, color, and exactness of structure all play their part in the loveliness of these pictures, and seem to combine all the visual qualities in which we as flower-loving people delight.

The script is written with clarity and understanding of the subject. The necessary fundamentals for executing flower and still life pictures is pleasingly told in all their phases. The authors have stated definitely the great importance of design, and all the other essential principles involved. The reading of these pages will inspire the reader to make further beauty out of the plant material he has at hand, no matter what section of the world he calls home for the rules are not limited to specific plant material.

In this day the average person who grows flowers wants to arrange them for a show or for the home, and in as pleasing and attractive a way as possible. It takes good material to make lovely arrangements, and for this reason I believe that this sort of art tends to increase the standards of horticulture. It is seldom that one wishes to use material that is not of a high standard horticulturally. Cut flowers in our American homes today play an important part in the scheme of interior decorations. Therefore it is all the more necessary that one should know the proper way to execute into beauty of design the everyday flowers to be placed in the home.

This publication will find a place in many a home where the beauties of nature are enjoyed. Its pages will ever speak of sunshine and sky, dawn and moonlight, cloud and wind, the sea, the glory of the garden, the radiance of the open field, the delicacy of the meadow and the fragrance of the woods. It challenges its readers to become skilled arrangers of flowers not alone for the satisfaction of their own souls, but for the enjoyment of all who pass their way.

NANNINE CLAY WALLIS
President National Council of State Garden Clubs

I

The Development of Flower Art

in America

Unfortunately the term "flower art" is a rather vague and indefinite one. As it has long been used by the commercial florists, it has too generally, almost universally, served to designate "set pieces" and baskets that were floral—but far from art!

As the term is employed in these pages, it may be defined as the art of arranging flowers in containers in such a way as to form a pleasing decorative design.

But even such a definition is quite inadequate because there is plenty of room for disagreement as to what is "pleasing"; and as much more as to what constitutes a "decorative design." However, most persons will agree as to when there has been a conscious effort to create a design—a thought-out, orderly placement of masses, lines, and colors in relation to each other—as contrasted, on the other hand, to materials that have been merely "stuck in" without any studied relationship. So that gives us at least a starting point.

In Western civilizations the arrangement of flowers has, at least until the very recent past, not been considered an art even remotely comparable to painting or etching. The massive bouquets of England and Holland, and the somewhat more delicately handled ones of France, held a place as minor decorations. The glorified versions of them to be found in the best flower paintings are probably far better, from the artistic viewpoint, than were the actual creations of their day.

In the Orient, however, it has been a different story. Especially in Japan, *rikwa*—the art of arranging flowers—held a place in national esteem but a little lower than that accorded the graphic arts.

PLATE 2. *PROPORTION TO SPACE*

Many flower show schedules call for arrangements in proportion to the space occupied—a requirement fulfilled quite perfectly by this composition in the Japanese tradition. The color harmony between plant materials, container, and stand is also particularly good.

Mrs. Ernest Brooks, Lawrence (N. Y.) Garden Club
International Flower Show, New York
Class: Flower picture. No restrictions, except proportion to
    space.

[3]

Brought originally from China, as have been so many other phases of Japanese culture, by the Buddhist priests, the art of flower arrangement took firm root in the soil of the Island Empire, and flourished amazingly. From the very beginning down to the present day, it has been associated with a religious and philosophic background of which it has always been considered an integral part.

It is this mystic symbolism which makes it so difficult for the Occidental mind to understand its full significance in the social consciousness of the Japanese—to comprehend how there can be separate and distinct schools of flower art all flourishing on one small group of islands no bigger than the state of California.

In America anything like a serious consideration of the art of arranging flowers is of comparatively recent origin. The turning point between the old-time, more or less haphazard bouquet, and what is now connoted by the term "arrangement" can be set just after John Taylor Arms, President of the American Society of Etchers, was asked to judge arrangements at the International Flower Show several years ago.

Mr. Arms' violent disagreement with the opinions of the other judges led to country-wide discussions of art as applied to flower arrangement, and for years he devoted much time to lecturing on this subject. Although Mr. Arms' emphasis was on pure design, with little attention to color, his efforts resulted in a marked revolution in the field of flower arrangement.

One of the immediate results of this serious study of the intriguing new art was, quite naturally, an investigation by its American devotees of what the Japanese had done and were doing. In many instances this was followed by a slavish attempt to imitate Japanese design without any real comprehension of its background or meaning, or knowledge of the Japanese technique. This was aided and abetted by dozens of amateur lecturers on the subject who knew little more of the subject than their listeners. A score or more hard and fast "rules" based on tenets of the Japanese schools were promulgated and enforced (under penalty of no awards if they were in the least violated!) where they did not at all apply.

The one most important development brought forth by all this effort to Americanize Japanese flower art was to make American arrangers "line conscious." Even though the pendulum swung too far in this direction, it was a much needed emphasis. Out of it has grown the modern line arrangement, which, while owing much to Japanese tradition, has broken the fetters of extreme Oriental classical limitations, and freed the imagination of the artist to dare and to execute new and bold designs.

In another respect, also, American arrangers have broken with the Japanese tradition. This is in the use of color. A glance through any of the many excellent Japanese books on flower arrangement will make evident the fact that here color is of secondary, often only of incidental, importance. Frequently it is introduced as a mere point of accent.

But Americans of the present day crave color— and lots of it. Its growing use has been conspicuous not only in the arts, and in interior decoration, but in all the contraptions of everyday use— even in the packages and wrapping of groceries and drugs. True, this cataract of color often is not well used; even in the "slick" magazines that purport to lead the way in showing us just how it should be done, there appear examples of room interiors, wall paper and draperies, and table settings that make anyone with a true feeling for color writhe in actual physical distress.

Despite all this, color, and ever more color, is in demand. Hence it was inevitable that in this country it should be accorded a position of more importance than the Japanese give it in their flower arrangements. During the last few years that tendency has been in marked evidence at flower shows, and the public has voiced its approval.

With the demand for more color—partly as a consequence of this demand, and partly as a revolt against the too frail and anemic arrangements that resulted from attempts to employ undigested precepts of the Japanese schools—there has come a demand for more robustness in our arrangements, for the use of more material in a design.

In this respect the lecture tours in this country of Constance Spry, the English authority, had a very wholesome effect. Entirely aside from the moot—and very moot it is!—question of the comparative merits of English and American flower arrangement, she was a breath of fresh air from over the downs blowing in through curtains too long laden with Japanese incense.

And so gradually, through many years of patient experimentation, trial and error, and the eventual victory of common sense over any slavish following of alien schools, there has been evolved in this country an art of flower arrangement which is distinctly different, distinctly new, distinctly American. It is still in a state of flux, a state of growth. It has not frozen into any fixed pattern; and let us hope it never will. Those who have led in its development—enthusiastic women scattered here and there over the country, who have taken their new art seriously, but not too much so—are still open minded, seeking progress, looking for the new but holding fast to that which has been found best in the old; devotees of an art which, while it has shed its swaddling clothes, is as yet but in its husky, buoyant infancy.

II

A Résumé of Design in Arrangement

$\mathcal{J}$UST WHAT IS a "flower arrangement"? How does it differ from a bouquet, or from flowers stuck haphazardly into a vase as a child might place them?

As has already been hinted, this term is not the easiest one in the world to define. But the essential difference between an arrangement and "just flowers" is that the former has an intentional design, a design which existed in the imagination of the arranger before it was given physical substance in materials, and thus represents a planned effort toward the creation of beauty.

[9]

Design, of course, may exist without intention, without any human mind or hand having played a part in its creation. The spreading, gracefully curved tendrils of an ivy against a stucco wall may form a lovely design but do not constitute an arrangement. On the wide window-sill before me as I write there is an aspiring young monstera plant which, with its deeply cut, large leaves and thick aerial roots clinging to rough cork bark, makes a bold and fascinating design. Near it is a philodendron in a piece of Mexican pottery, the peculiar burnt, bronzy color of which, "picked up" to perfection in the newly unfolded terminal leaves, makes as delicate and charming a design as one could wish. But neither of these, of course, is an arrangement. They are merely contributions to beauty made by nature, purely accidental as far as any human intent is concerned.

But these same materials, with little alteration, could be made the main features of arrangements. The Japanese are masters of the art of thus borrowing from nature, but no one could look at the simplest and most naturalistic Japanese arrangement without realizing immediately that it is no accident; that human intent and human skill lay

PLATE 3. *NATURE IN MINIATURE*

An example of the Japanese art which uses a single branch or a few twigs to represent a living tree, but always with a keen sense of proportion and balance.

Courtesy of Yamanaka & Company, New York, New York

[11]

behind its conception and execution. There is nothing remotely haphazard about the design.

What Is Design?

When we define a flower arrangement as being based on intentional design, we have still left unanswered the important question of what constitutes "design."

It is at just this point that many a beginning exhibitor at a flower show, and many a gardener who desires to arrange more effectively cut flowers in her living room, fails to comprehend the first principle of flower arrangement.

A design is the result of the bringing together of a number of component parts in such a way that the resulting whole has meaning and gives a sense of completeness and satisfaction.

It may be argued that a design which seems to have meaning for one person may hold none for another. This is quite true; and beyond this point the argument cannot be carried. Nevertheless there have been established, over a long period of time and by common consent, certain principles of good design now generally accepted.

PLATE 4. *SILHOUETTE*

A simple silhouette pattern against a harmonizing background—a type of arrangement particularly effective for home decoration, especially as the flowers can be replaced to give it long life.

Courtesy of Yamanaka & Company, New York, New York

[13]

On this basis it can be stated, as more or less of an axiom, that a good design has *composition, focus, balance,* and *unity.*

A design may rate so high in one of these factors that lower ratings in the others are overlooked, but in the best designs all of them will rank high.

THE ELEMENTAL PRINCIPLES OF DESIGN

What then do we mean by these terms—composition, focus, balance, unity? To attempt to define them briefly we may say that:

Composition is the relation of the parts to each other: the planned grouping of the parts which gives a result quite distinct from that which would be obtained if the same parts were merely put together in a haphazard manner.

Focus is the relation of the parts to the whole: the establishment of a center of interest which draws and holds the attention and to which the rest of the design is subservient. It is the bull's eye of the target upon which the eye fixes itself.

Balance is the relation of the parts to the axis of the design: the axis being an imaginary line, readily established by the eye in viewing a design, which cuts it into two halves. In most flower designs this axis extends vertically from the base to or near the highest point. Usually, but not always, it passes through the point of focus.

In a good design the apparent "weight" of the parts on either side of this axis line will balance each other, though the two sides may or may not be symmetrical.

Unity is the blending or harmonizing of the component parts of the design: the avoidance of the use of anything which would bring a jarring or discordant note into the design as a whole.

Over and above all these general principles there must be, as a guiding star, the artistic sense. It is quite possible to observe all of these principles meticulously in the creation of a design and still have the result absolutely flat and uninteresting, lacking in originality and character.

THE COMPONENT ELEMENTS OF THE ARRANGEMENT

Just as an artist works out his "arrangement" (a painting) in oils or water colors, so the maker of a flower arrangement starts with certain elements or parts which are to be grouped to make the finished whole. The artist—if he should chance to be painting an arrangement of flowers—

Elements of an Arrangement—
The Plant Material

would however start with certain advantages. He could create his own flowers, making them of any size, shape, or color he desired, and placing them exactly where he wanted them in his design. The flower arranger, however, must begin with parts or elements already fixed (once she has made her selection) as to form, size, and color. She does have the advantage of being able to work in three dimensions.

In any flower arrangement there are at least three parts or elements. These are:

PLATE 5. *SPRING THEME*

A bit of larch and a few azalea buds combine to effect this suggestion of a spring garden in Japanese naturalistic style.

Mrs. John R. Delafield, Millbrook (N. Y.) Garden Club
International Flower Show, New York
Class: Flower picture. No restrictions, except proportion to
space; 2nd prize.

[17]

3 Parts in arrangement

1 *The material:* cut flowers, foliage, seed pods, berries, fruits, or anything of a similar nature which strikes her fancy.

Elements of an Arrangement—
The Container

2 *The container:* the bowl, vase, or tray in which the materials are placed.

Elements of an Arrangement—
The Stand

3 *The background:* which always exists, whether or not it is especially provided to accompany the arrangement.

There may be also either or both of two other "parts." These are accessories such as small figures, a book, or a bit of jewelry (which is really merely supplementary material since it is not used in the arrangement proper); and stands (of wood, metal, jade, or whatnot) used under the container and, so far as the design goes, really a part of it.

Elements of an Arrangement—
The Accessories

Bases for containers of wood, metal, or other substances are now quite generally used, especially in arrangements done in the modern mode. Sometimes they add appreciably to the general effect obtained. In too many instances however, they are merely dragged in without rhyme or reason.

The most common mistake in the use, or rather abuse, of accessories is the employment of objects which play entirely too important a part in the general effect; or which in color, form, or atmosphere create a discord. Cleverly handled they may help to complete the design, as in the arrangement on page *11*. Sometimes they may be an integral part of it as in the lovely arrangement reproduced as the frontispiece of this volume.

The Completed Arrangement

Now each one of these parts, or elements, in the arrangement will have certain characteristics—at least five, to be exact. These are:

Shape: form, line, or silhouette.

Size: large or small, as related to other objects.

Mass or *tone:* the general quality of being comparatively light or dark.

PLATE 6. *EVERGREEN AND ONE KIND OF FLOWER*

A type of bold arrangement effective in a large room which the beginner can soon learn to do well, and which does not call for elaborate material. Over-obvious symmetrical balance is to be avoided.

Mrs. Edward H. Lebeis, Mamaroneck (N. Y.) Garden Club
International Flower Show, New York
Class: On a pedestal. Large arrangement of pine using red
    amaryllis for accent, tall dark container.

[21]

Color: a position in the chromatic circle (see page _89_).

Texture: smooth, rough, glossy, dull.

All of these rather dry details and definitions are mentioned at some length because, without an understanding of the terms being used, it is impossible to have any very intelligent discussion of the art of flower arrangement. With an understanding of these terms we can proceed to the next and more interesting step of attempting to analyze a good flower arrangement; taking it apart, so to speak, to see what makes it good.

And may we emphasize in passing that such a study of what goes to make up an attractive arrangement is of interest not merely to the flower show judge or the would-be prize winning exhibitor, but equally so to the amateur who wishes to make for her own living room arrangements attractive to herself, her family, and her friends. With no more time and experimenting than she would devote to familiarizing herself with new ideas in cooking, room decoration, or table setting, she can become at least reasonably proficient in this new art which adds its quota to the niceties of living.

Essentials in Good Design—
Composition

ANALYZING A SUCCESSFUL ARRANGEMENT

While a flower arrangement—even the simplest of line or silhouette arrangements in the Japanese manner—is three dimensional, let us for the sake

[23]

of simplicity, reduce our subject to a single plane, a flat surface; and simplify it further by eliminating color. Thus we can get, for instance, a silhouette outline or skeleton of the prize winning arrangement reproduced on page *37*.

The next step is to apply the elementary principles of design which we have already discussed to see how they fit this particular arrangement. These principles were, as you will recall, *composition*, *focus*, *balance* and *unity*.

Looking at this arrangement (above) it is at once evident that the first principle—that of *com-*

PLATE 7. *MODERN LINE*

This lovely clean-cut line arrangement, while revealing the effect of Japanese influence, illustrates how completely modern American arrangers have broken away from the fixed rules of the Japanese art.

Mrs. A. B. Thacher, Garden Club of the Oranges (N. J.)
International Flower Show, New York
Class: Color composition—monochromatic

[25]

position, or the ordered relation of the parts to each other—has been observed. The position of each flower and each leaf, it is obvious, has been carefully thought out so that the result will be a pleasing pattern.

In this connection it may be pointed out that the empty spaces between the various flowers and leaves are quite as much a part of the pattern as the flowers and foliage themselves. This is a fact which the beginner often overlooks.

Focus. As one looks at this arrangement it is equally obvious that there is a central point of interest, a "focus" to which the eye, unconsciously perhaps, but nevertheless inevitably, is led by the lines of the composition. In the other arrangements reproduced throughout this book such a focal point exists. In some of them, such as those shown on pages *21* and *99* it is obvious at first glance. In others it is more subtle; but in any good arrangement it is there.

Usually—as a scrutiny of the arrangement reproduced will show—the focus or center of interest in the arrangement is to be found slightly above the top of the container. Very often it is about one-third of the distance from the base of

Essentials in Good Design—
Focus

the container to the highest point of the arrangement. Concerning this, however, there is no set
rule. In arrangements that have one or two very
tall sprays, the focal point may appear to be lower
than it actually is. In such instances the *average*
height of the sprays is to be taken into consideration. See the arrangement shown on page *33*.

The focal point will also usually be found located on the central perpendicular axis of the arrangement. Here too, however, there is no set

Essentials in Good Design—
Balance

rule. In the arrangement reproduced on page *53* it will be noted that the focal point or center of interest is definitely to the right of the perpendicular axis.

PLATE 8. *FLORAL JEWEL-BOX*

While this arrangement of cryptanthus was entered in a rather specialized flower show class, it well illustrates the pleasing results that can be obtained with one species of flower and its own, or some other harmonizing foliage. Here the rich jewel-like effect of the whole arrangement is a fine achievement.

Mrs. John R. Delafield, Millbrook (N. Y.) Garden Club
International Flower Show, New York
Class: Cut plant material in low, open, or flat container. Design
to show different planes; 1st prize.

[29]

Balance. The relation of the various parts or elements of the arrangements to its central axis has also been nicely observed in the subject we have under consideration. The position of this axis has been indicated by a vertical line drawn through the arrangement. Obviously there is no apparent tendency of the arrangement to tip either to the right or to the left. The "weight" of the flowers and foliage on one side of the line balances that of the other side. This "weight" of course is a matter of visual appraisement only. Nevertheless its effect upon the observer is quite as real as though he could know the actual weight of the parts. Very dark flowers, for instance, appear to weigh more than light or white ones. We shall have more to say later concerning this matter of weight.

Unity. The harmonious blending of the component parts has also been observed in the arrangement under consideration. It will be noted that the general form of the flowers and of the container harmonize. This same harmony exists among the flowers themselves. The original, as may be seen by glancing at page *37* achieves unity not only in form but also in color and in texture.

Among the experts there is some dissension as to just what constitutes "unity" as far as the flowers themselves are concerned. Some extrem-

Essentials in Good Design—
Unity

ists hold that a tropical flower such as a calla should not be used with those of northern origin; that wildflowers and garden flowers if combined in an arrangement violate the principles of unity.

To the authors it has always seemed that this point of view is extreme and unjustified; that any plant material which contributes to the excellence of the design is admissible. Tropical flowers and wild flowers are made welcome in our gardens. In fact nearly everything we grow is, or was, "wild" somewhere before it was cultivated. Why then should any didactic rules to the contrary be made concerning arrangements? If a roadside weed or a greenhouse orchid helps your design, do not hesitate to use it. Here, as in so many other situations, commonsense and good taste will predicate what should or should not be attempted. If the use of weeds and orchids together gives an incongruous effect, to take an extreme case, the arranger should be the first to sense it, without the assistance of any rules. It is, however, by no means a foregone conclusion that the combination of a weed and an orchid must inevitably result in a jarring effect. Flowers of the native pitcher plant of our northern meadows, for instance, would probably combine very beautifully with certain types of orchids as might also the burning orange of the butterfly-weed or the peculiar blue of viper's bugloss.

PLATE 9. *FOR A ROSE BACKGROUND*

Simplicity—a few pussywillow twigs and white ranunculi. The half-opened buds both help the design and break the size contrast; while the touch of blue in the container adds greatly to the color interest.

Mrs. Elbert A. Bach, Flushing (L. I.) Garden Club
International Flower Show, New York
Class: Cut plant material in any container against a rose-colored
   background; 1st prize.

Two marked exceptions to the suggestions just given above are Japanese arrangements and certain types of theme arrangements. If one wishes to undertake arrangements in the Japanese manner, the rules should be strictly followed.

In a "theme" arrangement supposed to suggest Spring one, of course, would not use flowers normally blooming in summer or not hardy in the locality. In an arrangement designed to suggest coolness, obviously it would be inappropriate to use flowers of red or other warm hues. Commonsense, again, must be the arbiter.

III

Planning the Arrangement

 *I*T IS ONE THING, however, to study a successful arrangement and see how it complies with certain general principles and quite another to put
one together. Analysis is always easier than syn-
thesis.

An excellent process for the beginner is to attempt to recreate in general effect, if not in every
detail, an arrangement that has been seen and ad-
mired. This, however, should be considered
merely as practice work; finger exercises in technique. Above all, one should avoid, when making an arrangement for a flower show, the mis-

Plant Material Stuck in a Container—
No Design

take so common to many beginners, that is, imitating something which has been seen elsewhere.

We have already defined the four basic factors which go to make up good design in an arrangement: *composition, focus, balance* and *unity*. Before attempting to put an arrangement together further consideration of each of these is necessary. To reduce this study to elementary terms, let us assume that we have some simple cut flower material and a container—to be specific, calla lilies, their buds and foliage, and a shallow bowl. These are the elements or parts from which our flower arrangement is to be constructed.

PLATE 10. *ACCENT ON SPACES*

*In line arrangements the spaces between stems, foliage, and flowers are as
carefully considered as the placement of the materials. The importance
of this factor is well shown in this arrangement.*

Mrs. Paul Sturtevant, Bedford (N. Y.) Garden Club
International Flower Show, New York
Class: Flower picture. No restrictions except proportion to
   space; 3rd prize.

Composition. It is at once evident that flowers and foliage may be placed in the bowl in an unlimited number of ways.

If they are merely stuck in, as a child may place them, it is at once apparent that the result does

Poor Design—
No Balance or Focal Point

not give any sense of composition, of a planned and thought-out relationship. (See page *36*.)

They may, however, be so placed that such a planned relationship becomes evident. But it does not follow that the resulting composition will be a pleasing one. The veriest tyro in the art of flower arrangement would not be satisfied with the way these flowers have been grouped on page *38*, although they form a composition of a sort.

Focus. For one thing there is no central point of interest—no focus—to catch and hold the eye. So let us try again, to see if this fault can be cor-

Better—
Balance, but no Focal Point

rected. Then we might get an arrangement like the one shown on page *40*. But it is obvious that the arrangement is still far from satisfactory. A central point of interest, or focal point, has been obtained by bringing the stems together, but the general effect is disquieting and unsatisfactory. The whole thing appears lop-sided and in immi-

Improved—
Focal Point Has Been Added

nent danger of falling over. In other words the composition is lacking in balance.

Balance. So once again we shift our flowers and foliage around to try to correct this fault. A little experimenting will show that it can be done in either one of two ways. The easiest way is to make a *symmetrical* arrangement in which the flowers and foliage on one side of an imaginary center line or axis approximately duplicate those on the other. (See page *43*.) The other way is to so distribute the flowers and foliage that the apparent "weight" of the material on one side of

PLATE II. *BASKET CONTAINER*

Basket and bamboo containers, used in many Japanese arrangements, find favor with many American flower lovers, often with less success than has been achieved in this simple combination of narcissi, rhododendron leaves, and broom.

Mrs. Frederick W. Lewis, Little Neck (L. I.) Garden Club
Daffodil Show of the Horticultural Society of New York
Class: Basket of narcissi arranged for effect; 1st prize.

the center line or axis will balance those on the other even though the two sides are entirely different. This is termed *asymmetrical* balance. (See page *44*.)

Still Better

It is possible to make a symmetrically balanced arrangement that is interesting and pleasing. If well done, such compositions are often strikingly effective. In general, however, it will be found that asymmetrical balance gives a much more interesting result. Certainly this is true of arrangements for the home which are to be kept and looked at for a number of days. The difference between symmetrical and asymmetrical balance is well illustrated in the color reproductions on page *57* where the same container has been used. Other good examples of symmetrical balance will be found on pages *105* and *131*.

Symmetrical Balance

We have made the statement that in an asymmetrically balanced arrangement the apparent weight of the flowers and foliage on one side of the central axis should equal that on the other. It is interesting to determine just what gives them weight. This is not actual weight measured in

Asymmetrical Balance

pounds and ounces but the *impression* of weight that is obtained by the materials used and their location in the arrangement.

Three general principles which any beginner can easily keep in mind apply here, and once memorized they will be of great help to the artist with flowers in making well-balanced arrangements. The three principles are:

1. The farther away from an imaginary center line a flower, bud, leaf, or other unit of material is placed, the greater is its apparent weight.

PLATE 12. *SPRING CRESCENT*

The circular motif called for in the schedule is carried out not only in the design but also in the plant material, the container, and the stand, the reverse curves of the legs of which add an original note. The darker flower buds, picking up the tone of the container, are just enough to avoid monotony.

Mrs. Earle S. Rhine, South Orange (N. J.) Garden Club
International Flower Show, New York
Class: Arrangement based on circular design, 1st prize.

2. The higher above the container a unit of material is placed in the arrangement, the greater its apparent weight.

Balance—Figure 1

3. The darker the color of a flower or other unit of material, the greater its apparent weight. (A dark red rose may actually weigh no more than a pure white one of the same size but visually it is much heavier.) The accompanying diagrams help to illustrate these points.

[46]

Quite apart from its apparent weight, due to any of the conditions suggested above, a flower may have an *interest value* that sets it apart from other material in the arrangement. This interest value, though more subtle in nature, is a factor to be considered in securing a perfect balance.

A single blossom, a flowering spray, or other plant material that is extraordinary in size, in form, or in color concentrates attention upon it-

Balance—Figure 2   Balance—Figure 3

self and therefore requires particularly careful placement.

Size emphasis is illustrated by the amaryllis in the arrangement on page 37. Neither in form nor

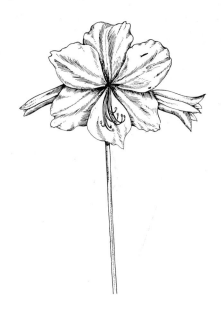

Emphasis — Size

in color is it arresting, but its size causes it to dominate the entire arrangement.

Form emphasis is shown by the banana blossom in the arrangement on page 109 and by the cactus "spoons" on page 141. (Incidentally, it is inter-

PLATE 13. *MODERN MASS*

In the modern form of the old mass arrangement there is a general "loosening up" of the plant material, so that individual flowers and foliage sprays show to advantage. It is really a combination of line and mass.

Mrs. Langdon Lee, The Weeders, Philadelphia, Pennsylvania
International Flower Show, New York
Class: Flower picture. No restrictions except proportion to
    space.

esting to note in all three of these arrangements how effectively the pattern of the dominating feature in the plant material has been repeated in the

Emphasis—Form

container. The shape of the petals of the amaryllis, and the form of the banana blossom might almost have been used as models for the vases which hold them.)

Color emphasis often is combined with striking form or unusual size, but not always. The little florets on a spray of euphorbia, for instance, be-

[50]

come a dominating point of interest in any arrangement in which they are used simply because
of their burning orange color.

Emphasis — Color

In some instances we get a combination of unusual size, form, and color all in the same flower,
and then everything else has to take a back seat.
The strelitzia or Bird-of-Paradise flower is per-

[51]

Emphasis—
A Combination of Size, Form, and Color

haps the most striking example of such a combination. It is used in the arrangements shown on
pages *99* and *131*.

So far we have been discussing balance within
the arrangement itself, but the container in which
the flowers are placed and the base which supports the container (if one is used) are also an

PLATE 14. *FRENCH INFLUENCE*

A modern mass arrangement in the French manner. The touch of green foliage and the dark shade of blue of the base save the color scheme from being too tritely obvious.

Miss Nellie Huh, New Rochelle (N. Y.) Garden Club
Judges' Course of the Federated Garden Clubs of New York State
Class: An arrangement using complementary colors.

[53]

integral part of the arrangement and affect not only the design but its apparent balance.

No matter how carefully balanced the flowers and foliage in an arrangement may be, apparent instability will result if they are too high in

Balance in Container

Unbalanced   Improved   Better

proportion to the container; if they are too bulky in proportion to the container; or if they are in the wrong position in the container.

The position of the flowers in the container is of particular importance when a low bowl, dish, Japanese "boat," or anything similar is used. The Japanese are masters in achieving effects of delicate but accurate balance by providing perfect placement of plant material in relation to the container. A study of good examples of Japanese flower art will greatly assist the beginner in mastering this point in technique. Examples of proper placement are to be found in the arrangements on pages *13* and *33*.

Unity. By no means the least important of the elements of good design to be discussed here is unity, the harmonious blending of the component parts of the arrangement.

Unity is the cement which holds the arrangement together. No matter how good the design, focus, and balance may be, without unity the result must fail to be satisfactory and often is aggressively displeasing even to the observer who does not realize just what is wrong.

Unity must begin with the conception or idea back of the arrangement. It may be a definite thought or emotion that the designer wishes to express (as in the arrangements on pages *163* and *167*) or it may apply to the simplest bouquet, like those shown on pages *203* and *207*. It is the successful employment of this principle of unity, more than any of the other three, that usually marks the difference between the mediocre and the really excellent arrangement.

The first step in achieving unity is to negotiate a happy marriage between the container and the plant material used. Both form and color must be considered. If we can go a step further and achieve such a unity in that more subtle thing called spirit or atmosphere, so much the better. A negative example may help to illustrate this point: one would not think for instance of using a characteristically Japanese container for a mass arrangement even though its shape were suitable and the coloring quite perfect for the flowers to be used. Good examples of unity of spirit between the container and the plant material will be found in the arrangements on pages *155* and *233*.

Texture. This, too, is an important factor to watch for in securing unity between the container and the material. In a closely contested class many an arrangement has finally received the blue ribbon because of excellence in the textural relationship between the container and the plant material. Those who specialize in making arrangements for the more important flower shows often have special containers made in order to obtain just the texture and the color desired. The woman who is making arrangements for her

PLATE 15. *BALANCES*

*These two arrangements, in identical containers, exemplify the difference
between asymmetrical and symmetrical balance in design, though neither are
extreme examples. They also show the wide range in treatment possible in
modern mass arrangements.*

Mrs. Robert R. Kearfott, Mamaroneck (N. Y.) Garden Club *and*
Mrs. Roy M. Lincoln, Port Washington (L. I.) Garden Club
Judges' Course of the Federated Garden Clubs of New York State
Class: Asymmetrical and symmetrical massed arrangements in
    identical containers.

home or for a local show usually cannot go to this expense and trouble. Often, however, an old container can be resurfaced either with a stain or a heavy-bodied paint to give the texture desired at a very trifling expense for the materials required.

In any event, a study of good arrangements, with particular attention to the harmony between the container and the plant material, will be of great assistance in enabling even the beginner to select the vase, bowl, bottle, or jug in keeping with her flowers and foliage.

The didactic rules advanced by some experts that only certain materials—such as glass or silver—should be used with certain flowers is mere poppycock. It may be perfectly true that zinnias usually look well in Mexican pottery or roses in silver, but the very fact that these combinations are so frequently seen is all the more reason for trying to find something else that will give an equally pleasing effect.

PUTTING THE ARRANGEMENT TOGETHER

It is not an easy matter for the beginner at flower arrangement to keep in mind, during her first few attempts, all of the considerations we have been discussing. With a little practice, however, she will soon find herself almost unconsciously being guided by them. The mistakes

A Rough Sketch May Help in
Visualizing the Proposed Arrangement

that escaped detection at first will become instantly obvious.

The steps followed in putting an arrangement together are usually six:

1. Getting the construction or mental picture of what is to be aimed at. This may either be very definite or just a general idea. Usually, but not always, the more clearly this mental picture can be brought into sharp focus before the actual work of construction is begun, the better the

Remove the Surplus!
Original Form   Trimmed to Desired Lines

result will be. In order to help get a very definite mental image, some designers make a rough sketch showing the relationship between the container and the plant material and the main lines to be followed in arranging the latter. Whether or not such an attempt to "get things down in black and white" will prove helpful depends entirely upon the temperament of the individual.

[60]

PLATE 16. *TRIAD COLOR SCHEME*

*Shades and tones of red, green, and blue are here combined to produce a
charming tetrad arrangement in which a strong focal point has been secured
without giving it bull's-eye prominence.*

Mrs. William Whitney, Garden City-Hempstead (L. I.) Community Club
Judges' Course of the Federated Garden Clubs of New York State
Class: Composition using any cut plant material, not dried; 2nd prize.

2. *Selecting the materials and the container.* Usually in working out a mental concept of the form the arrangement is to take, either the container or the plant material serves as the starting point. The problem then is to select the other.

Making an Arrangement—
Determine the Main Lines

In bringing cut flowers from the garden for indoor decoration one usually starts with the flowers and selects from such containers as may be available the one that will be most suitable. In making show pieces, as often as not, the container is the first thing decided upon, and then the search for suitable plant material begins. If accessories or a special background are to be employed, they may be decided upon at this time or left until the arrangement has been completed. In providing decorations for the home such

Making an Arrangement—
Provide Focal Point of Interest

adjuncts must be used with great caution or they will seem overpretentious.

3. Building the skeleton. In most modern arrangements, even comparatively simple ones for the home, certain strongly accented lines and curves will predominate. These form the skele-

ton of the finished arrangement and their positions are determined and made sufficiently secure
so that they will not be disarranged before minor
details are filled in. (See remarks on mechanical
details in Chapter VI.

Making an Arrangement—
Add Supplementary Lines

At this point it is well to back a few feet away
from the prospective work of art and give it a
careful visual checking up to see if it satisfies the
general principles of design—composition, focus,
balance and unity. Changes can readily be made
at this point which, if left until later, may wreck
the whole thing.

[64]

PLATE 17. *CONTAINER AND MATERIAL HARMONY*

This clean-cut mass arrangement with a bold line silhouette is an excellent example of how important a part the container and base can play in the ensemble. Both their color and texture have been perfectly picked up in the bronze rubber plant foliage.

Mrs. Ralph V. Magoffin, Associate Member of the Federated
  Garden Clubs of New York State
Judges' Course of the Federated Garden Clubs of New York State
Class: Composition using any cut plant material, not dried, 1st
  prize.

4. Filling in the details. Such secondary or supplementary lines or masses as are desired may now be added. It is just at this point that the beginner is most likely to go wrong, for the

Making an Arrangement—
Finish the Details

temptation to put in too much is always strong. What is left out is quite as important as what is put in. The skillful removal of leaves and twigs or small branches may save confusion and "cross lines," particularly at the base of the arrangement where the various stems are brought together and where there should be a strong, clearly defined focal point. Examples of such restraint will be found in the reproductions on pages *17* and *195*.

5. Making the final check-up. When the arrangement has been completed the flower artist must change her role and turn from creator to critic. This involves making a rather difficult mental somersault which is *not* done with the greatest of ease, but which, nevertheless, is important if the arranger is to correct her own mistakes instead of leaving them to be discovered by the judges at a flower show, or by friends or visitors if it is a home piece.

Up to this point we have been considering the design of flower arrangement in terms of black and white, for the silhouette effects of lines and masses form the basis of design. But in arrangements with plant material (even dried material) another vital factor is always present. This is *color*. Without at least a rudimentary understanding of the principles that govern the successful use of color, the flower arranger is at a great disadvantage.

It is quite true that a native sense of color values and harmonies may pull one through, just as some persons can play musical compositions by ear. But even those so fortunate as to possess such a gift will find helpful a rudimentary understanding of color. So our next step is to attempt to achieve such an understanding.

IV

A Basis for Color Study

To BEGIN any discussion of color—even an elementary one "in words of one syllable"—it is essential as a first step to get rid of some common misconceptions.

In the first place there is no such thing as color in the sense in which it is ordinarily conceived. What we know as color is a *sensation* resulting from light waves of varying lengths striking upon the retina of the eye and which is then conveyed to the brain through the nerve mechanism associated with the retina. Just as atmospheric waves of a given frequency produce a certain sound, so light waves of a given frequency produce the sensation which we describe as a particular color. And just as some atmospheric waves or vibrations are of so high or so low a pitch that the human ear cannot register them, so light waves above or below a very limited scale of frequencies are not registered by the human eye. At one end of the scale these invisible light waves are known as the infra-red rays, and at the other as the ultra-violet rays.

The Spectrum Colors

In between these two are the colors, or hues, which the human eye can distinguish. They blend into each other in such a way that it is not possible to say just where one ends and the other begins. Nevertheless there are seven which persons of normal vision can readily distinguish. These are red, orange, yellow, green, blue, indigo (or ultra-marine indigo), and violet.

As any school boy or school girl knows, a ray of sunlight, if broken up by being passed through a prism, will produce a band of color in which these hues appear in the order given. This band

PLATE 18. *À LA GAUGUIN*

An arrangement to suggest the color technique of a famous painter—a problem for the advanced student, but interesting also to the ambitious amateur.

Mrs. George W. Both, Scarsdale (N. Y.) Garden Club
International Flower Show, New York
Class: Invitation—Still life to suggest the color of Paul Gauguin; special award.

is known as the spectrum, and the seven distinct hues which make it up, as the spectrum hues (or colors).

If they are now passed through another prism these rays of light of varying wave lengths (which we see as colors) will be reunited and appear again as white light.

It is obvious, then, that we have colors entirely disassociated from solid physical objects. The rainbow in the sky does not exist there as a material arch; it is the result of the breaking up of sunbeams into the hues of the spectrum as they pass through raindrops which serve the same purpose as the prism in the experiment described above.

The colors, or hues, with which we deal in most phases of life, however, are not spectrum hues obtained from direct sunlight. When we speak of a red book, a brown piece of cloth, or a pink rose petal, we are dealing with color effects produced by light waves *reflected from surfaces*. The reason why these surfaces appear to be of different hues is because each such surface reflects light waves of a certain frequency while absorbing others with higher or lower wave lengths.

Surfaces which *reflect* all of the light waves (visible to the human eye) we describe as being white; those which *absorb* all of the light waves as black (the absence of all hue or color).

SOME ELEMENTARY EXPERIMENTS

Color, as we experience it in our everyday contact, is largely the result of the use of certain pigments employed in manufacturing. With paint or varnish the natural hues of wood are altered to give us any desired color. By the application of dyes the comparative white of bleached cotton or the natural tan of silk is changed to any one of hundreds of colors.

An important fact in relation to any study of color is that spectrum hues, obtained directly from light, have characteristics differing from hues produced by pigments. Certain pairs of the spectrum hues when combined produce white. These are called "complementary" hues. Yellow light and blue light are complementary, and when combined produce white. But if pigments of the same yellow and blue are combined the resultant hue is green!

Then, too, the *eye* plays tricks in relation to color. A band of yellow, for instance, with a band of green on either side of it will appear to be a quite different hue from the same band of yellow with a band of blue on either side of it. Almost everyone at some time or other has tried the simple but rather startling experiment of gazing intently at a spot of color for several moments and then, upon suddenly closing the eyes, being able to "see" not the color that he had been looking at, but its complement or opposite.

It is evident, then, that there are three quite distinct types of color impression: those received from direct light waves; those received from pigments, by reflected light rays; and those due to visual phenomena caused by the eye and the brain.

Much of the confusion existing in discussions of color is due to a failure to distinguish among these three fields, and to statements made concerning one which do not apply to the others.

How Colors Are Made Up

The average person of normal color vision can readily distinguish many hundreds of colors.

PLATE 19. *CÉZANNE INSPIRES*

*Here Cézanne has supplied the inspiration for color harmony, which is
extended to the background and base cloth in a subdued but rich creation.
The artist's characteristic use of geometric patterns has been followed.*

Mrs. Roy M. Lincoln, Port Washington (L. I.) Garden Club
International Flower Show, New York
Class: Invitation—Still life to suggest the color of Paul Cézanne;
    special award.

Some authorities put the figures in the thousands. It is difficult for the layman to believe that this vast number of different colors can be made up from a few primary colors plus black and white, although the colors depicted in the reproductions in this book (produced by the process known as four-color printing) have been made up by combinations of yellow, red, blue, and black ink.

Authorities differ as to just how many primary colors there are, but that does not concern us here. Anyone who will take the trouble to experiment with a few tubes of paint can readily find out that a mixture of blue and yellow will give him green; red and yellow will produce orange; red and blue, purple; and so on.

If, instead of making half-and-half mixtures of these various pigments, the experimenter tries different proportions, he will, of course, get results quite different from those obtained before. A mixture of two-thirds yellow and one-third blue for instance will give a yellowish green. Reversing the proportions will give a bluish green.

There is, however, another, and quite different, respect in which colors differ from each other. If

PLATE 20. *AFRIC SPLENDOR*

*Flowers, fruit, and foliage of plants of South African origin are composed
in a way to suggest the variety and opulence of a tropical land, the spear-
shaped leaf being a master touch.*

Mrs. Francis F. Merriam, Montclair (N. J.) Garden Club
International Flower Show, New York
Class: Primitive splendor, South Africa; 3rd prize.

the experimenter will take any one of the original hues with which he started (or one of those obtained by mixing them) and add to it black or white in varying amounts, he will get an entirely new range of colors which he could not before obtain, no matter in what proportions he mixed his pigments. By adding both black and white (gray) he gets still another range.

THE DIMENSIONS OF COLOR

It becomes evident, then, that whatever hue we start with can be changed in any one of *three* directions merely by the addition of black, white or gray—a fact that can be visualized by a very simple diagram.

Unfortunately the color theorists and experts have used no standardized system of nomenclature. Terms employed by one have been used by another to express something entirely different. To us it seems that the terminology employed by Faber Birren is the most logical so far suggested and the most readily comprehended by the layman. We have therefore used it in these pages in the belief that it will help to clarify much of the confusion in the usual discussion of color. (See "color nomenclature" page *82.*)

According to the system of nomenclature used by Birren any pure hue (or color) to which black

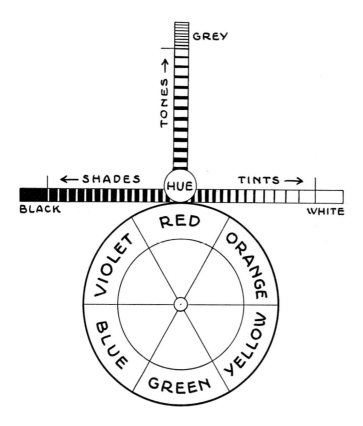

The Dimensions of Color

is added produces a *shade* of that hue; the addition of white produces a *tint;* and the addition of gray produces a *tone.*

These shades, tints, and tones will, of course, vary progressively with the amount of black, white, or gray added to the original hue.

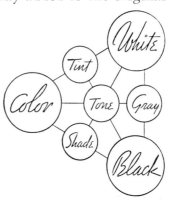

The Color Triangle

These relationships, represented in the form of a diagram, give us the Birren "color triangle."

It is thus obvious that any given hue can be varied—by the addition of black, white or gray—to give as many shades or tones as the eye can distinguish. For practical purposes Birren has worked these out in a series of charts, one of which is reproduced here. Those interested will find the others in his *The American Colorist.*

CHART OF MONO-
CHROMATIC HARMONIES

The various color modifications charted on this diagram have been worked out on a scientific basis using a special mathematical formula. It will be noted that the tints, shades, and tones show perfect analogy in all directions—horizontally, vertically, or diagonally across the chart.

COLOR NOMENCLATURE

As already implied, discussion in the field of color has been greatly handicapped by the indiscriminate use of terms that either had no definite and specific meaning, or were used in one sense by some authors or lecturers and in another by others. An attempt to define some of these terms may help to clarify the situation.

Color (used generically). The whole subject of the spectrum; of pigment hues, their variations, and of their uses.

Color (used specifically). Designates any particular hue, such as blue, red, or orange or—less accurately— designating shades, tints or tones of such hues.

Spectrum. The band of pure colors obtained by passing sunlight through a prism.

Fundamental colors. The colors of the spectrum, six or seven in number, according to different authorities: they are red, orange, yellow, green, blue (indigo or purple) and violet.

Primary colors. The basic colors (red, yellow and blue, or otherwise, according to the "system" used) combinations of which give the remaining or intermediary colors.

Secondary or Intermediary colors. Those between the primaries, such as orange, purple and violet.

Hue. A full strength color in the spectrum or the color circle (formerly used to distinguish intermediary colors such as orange or magenta from the primary colors).

Shade. A hue made darker, as by the addition of black.

Tint. A hue made lighter, as by the addition of white.

Tone. A hue made duller, as by the addition of gray.

Complementary colors. Opposites on the color circle, which combine into white or neutral (medium) gray.

Chroma. "The strength of a color" (whatever that means!).

Brilliance
Luminosity
Pitch
} The degree of approach to pure color or hue, but often confused with illumination and texture, two other factors involved. Increased light, or a shiny surface, step up the *apparent* degree of pureness.

Saturated color
Pure color
} Less definite synonyms for hue.

Intensity
Value
Notan
} "Indicating the percentage of black and white"; less definite than shade, tone and tint.

Scale (chromatic scale). A series of hues (or of shades, tones or tints) in gradual transition: the spectrum, the color circle, or a segment of the color circle, is such a scale.

Although in this brief discussion it has been possible merely to touch a few of the high spots in connection with the underlying principles of color, those who have the leisure and the inclination to delve into it further will find it a most fascinating field. The more one learns about it, the keener will be the pleasure which the individual can derive from color in general. But we must pass on from the generalities we have been considering to the more specific question of the part that color can play in making attractive flower arrangements.

V

Theory of Color Uses

*A*s there are harmonies and discords in music (the combination of sounds), so there are harmonies and discords in combinations of color. And as in music, some persons are much more sensitive than others to these harmonies and discords. A "sense of color" cannot be imparted; like a sense of harmony in music or a sense of design, it is something with which the individual, to a greater or lesser degree, is born. Nevertheless, an understanding of the subject can help develop this sense. As in the case of design, an understanding of a few basic principles concerning color will greatly assist the flower arranger both to do better work herself and to appreciate and enjoy good work done by others.

So far in our discussion of color we have been concerned with its *physical* basis. In making practical use of color, however, it is the *psychological* basis that counts. We do not, for example, speak of red as being a "warm" color because we believe it is of a higher temperature than such "cool" colors as blue or green; yet psychologically these differences do exist. A "blue" electric spark may be many times hotter than a "red" flame, but we cannot get away from the psychological associations that have been built up during thousands of years of racial experience.

In the same way, by general consent, we find some combinations of color harmonious and others discordant. It may be said that this is a matter of personal taste. Nevertheless the general rule holds true. The colored girl who went into a dress shop and informed the saleswoman she was looking for "something simple and quiet—jist red, green, and yaller" would have found herself, in any average group, so much in the minority concerning the point of view on

PLATE 21. *RICH COLORING*

*Rich in coloring as a Rembrandt or a Frans Hals, this very original composition of dried plant material won acclaim from experts and amateurs alike.
In flower arrangement as in other arts there is always room for a new idea.*

Mrs. Joseph Gazzam, Larchmont (N. Y.) Garden Club
Judges' Course of the Federated Garden Clubs of New York State
Class: Composition with dried material.

color that her opinion would not have carried much weight.

The Color Circle

As has previously been pointed out, the colors with which we come into daily contact are not the pure hues found in the spectrum, but those made up from combinations of pigments of various sorts. The same thing is true of colors found in flowers, very few of which even approximate the hues of the spectrum.

For use in the study and the application of color there have been made up by various investigators chromatic or color circles. In these circles the hues shown are in the same sequence as those of the spectrum. The arrangement differs however in the number of hues into which the color circle is divided, and in their relation to each other. In general the object has been to obtain such a disposition of the hues in the circle that those *directly opposite* each other would be supplementary—that is, when mixed together they would produce a neutral gray. It must be remembered that we are dealing with pigments.

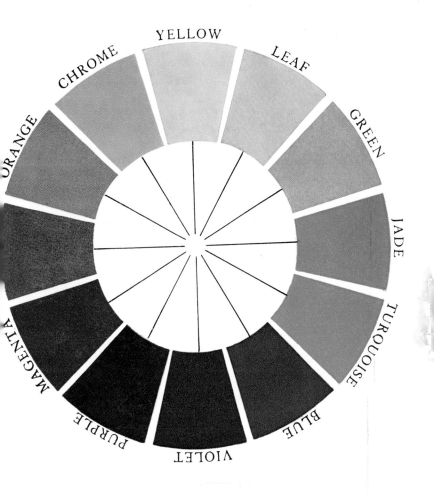

YELLOW
LEAF
CHROME
GREEN
ORANGE
JADE
MAGENTA
TURQUOISE
PURPLE
BLUE
VIOLET

THE COLOR CIRCLE

The color standards shown on this chart have been balanced in accordance with visual and psychological laws of color. The sequence from hue to hue around the circle offers a complete circuit of the spectrum. The opposite pairs are direct visual complements and will cancel into neutral gray when mixed.

[89]

Of the many chromatic or color circles so devised one of the easiest to use and the most accurately balanced is that of Faber Birren which is reproduced herewith.

In looking at the sequence of hues shown, any observer will feel that they differ in the psychological effects they produce.

First of all, some of them suggest warmth and others coolness. Red, instinctively associated with fire, gives very definitely the effect of warmth; jade, suggesting almost as instinctively a curling wave or a cavern under the sea, carries with it the effect of coolness. Hues adjacent to red and to jade also suggest warmth and coolness, but in diminishing degree as they approach yellow and violet. Leaf and purple (on the Birren circle) mark the dividing lines between the warm and the cool hues.

In still another respect this handful of hues differ in their psychological effect. The warmest hues—red, orange and magenta—are *advancing* in character; they seem to come at you; they are aggressive. All of the cool hues, on the contrary, from leaf to violet, are retiring, *receding*. They seem to suggest distance, a fact which the land-

PLATE 22. *AUTUMN THEME*

Suggestion of the summer's close is conveyed by this grouping of dahlias, fruits, and colored foliage. The arrangement is a bit weak, tending to "break in two" at the center—undoubtedly a point of interest to the quizzical duck with the expression of a flower show judge.

Mrs. George Loflund, Forest Hills, Long Island
Autumn Show of the Horticultural Society of New York
Class: Still life with autumn flowers and fruits; 1st prize.

[91]

scape architect often takes advantage of in planning a garden where space is limited.

Yellow, with its connotation of sunshine, is universally recognized as the most cheerful of hues. Blue and violet to many persons are actually physically depressing. Equally well recognized is the quieting or tranquilizing effect of green and yellow-green (leaf).

COLOR HARMONIES

Certain rather definite combinations of hues (or of shades, tints, or tones) are, to the average person, more pleasing than others. These combinations we speak of as color harmonies. The creator of flower arrangements who learns what these combinations are will save herself many mistakes. Such rules can, of course, be broken— sometimes successfully—but in general it is safer to work within their bounds.

Monochromatic Harmony. The simplest and easiest pattern for obtaining a color harmony is to use only one hue, and supplement this with shades, tints, and tones of the same hue. But while such a straight-line or one-family harmony is almost sure to be pleasing, it carries with it the danger of becoming monotonous; of lacking character, "punch." In color monochromatic harmony in an arrangement is comparable to symmetrical balance in design.

Analogous Harmony. More interesting, and a little more difficult to achieve, is the analogous harmony in which adjoining hues on the color circle (such as red, orange, and chrome, or blue, violet, and turquoise) are used together. Such combinations are particularly effective in emotional quality because the warmth or coolness, cheerfulness or tranquility of the principal hue employed is re-enforced and intensified by its supporting neighbors.

Complementary Harmony. In the two types of color combinations discussed above, harmony is secured by the association of the *like*. In complementary harmonies we have the marriage of the *unlike;* color combinations based on contrasts. These are of four types: direct complements; dual or "split"complements; triads, in which three hues equidistant from each other around the color circle are used; and tetrads, in which four hues equidistant around the color circle are employed.

[93]

Harmonies based on contrast are quite different in their general effect from those based on similarity or likeness. They are vivid and arresting; they may even be startling. Yet, if they are well done, there is no sense of a lack of harmony. This principle is well illustrated in the reproduction on page *125*.

Many of our common flowers present familiar examples of the effectiveness of strong contrasts. The yellow and violet of the common wild aster is a combination which, in somewhat varying hues, also appears in erigeron, purple crocus and the tulip Louis IV, one of the most popular of all varieties. The red and yellow of the common eastern wild columbine; the blue and pure white of some of the cultivated columbine hybrids; the yellow rings and dark centers of annual chrysanthemums; and the rich purples and reds of fuchsias all add their testimony to the effectiveness of strong contrasts in floral hues. The humble pansy with its frequently startling, but never displeasing, combinations of color is perhaps the best example of all.

The effect which flowers of this general type have upon the observer is perceptibly different

COMPLEMENTARY COLORS

This study in color combination was designed to illustrate the use of "direct opposites" or complementary colors.

Mrs. F. S. Rathbone, Mamaroneck (N. Y.) Garden Club
Judges' Course of the Federated Garden Clubs of New York State
Class: An arrangement using complementary colors.

from that produced by blooms which exemplify harmony through analogy or similarity in their hues. To say that they are more startling is perhaps to employ too strong a word, but the difference does exist. Some flowers conspicuous for analogous coloration are those with blending hues, shades, and tints of orange and yellow such as the popular "salmon" and "coral" hybrid tea roses, montbretias, geums, and some of the tritomas. It is interesting to note that the hues of most of the flowers with analogous coloring are in the warm or advancing group, as though this were nature's method for compensating them for the lack of contrast in their coloring. There are, however, exceptions to this general rule. One of these is the cheerful and sunny, but not at all flamboyant, Golden Cup or Mexican Tulip Poppy (*Hunnemannia fumariaefolia*) a symphony in rather pale yellow and yellowish gray-green in the foliage. (And incidentally it is a splendid flower for cutting, more substantial and longer lasting than the more commonly grown types of poppies.) An even more striking illustration of the "quiet" type of analogous coloring in flowers is the blue hardy salvia (*Salvia farinacea*).

These facts concerning the coloring of flowers have been presented in some detail because they have a very direct bearing on the handling of color in flower arrangement. From them many helpful suggestions may be obtained. One noted painter of flowers, in working out his color scheme for a picture, always looks to the flower itself, or to the plant on which it grows, to give him his cue as to what colors to use for background, container, or other objects in his painting. His contention is that if one looks carefully enough it will be found that nature has already provided the color scheme, although some of the factors may be present in but small areas such as the coloring of an anther or a stamen, the sheaf of the unopened bud, an unfolding leaf, or the reverse side of petals or foliage.

Direct Complement Harmonies. As already explained the complementary harmonies—harmony by contrast—are of four general types: direct complements, split complements, triads, and tetrads.

Of these the direct complement, or the combination of two hues directly opposite on the color circle, (such as yellow and violet or jade and red; see page *89*) are by far the easiest to secure. As pointed out in the discussion of the coloration of flowers these direct complements are the most dramatic, sometimes almost startling. By the same token, however, they are also the most obvious. For instance one so often sees yellow flowers, such as yellow roses, placed in a blue container or photographed against a blue background, that much of the natural appeal of such a combination is inevitably lost. Indeed, it eventually reaches the point where there is almost instinctively an unfavorable reaction on the part of the observer. How often has any flower show judge heard—or made!—the remark, "That's been done a thousand times before. Why couldn't she have tried something more original?"

Under some conditions however, a strikingly dramatic and direct contrast in the color scheme just suits the conditions to be met. Arrangements which must be viewed from a considerable distance, such as those at the end of a very large room, in a church, or in a public meeting place, are most effective if a strong direct contrast or complement is used as the basic color scheme.

The most dramatic of direct complementary color schemes are secured when the contrast is

PLATE 24. *MODERN*

Modern as tomorrow is this stunning design in which the strongly accented color rhythm is insistent as the beat of a tom-tom, while the contrasting focal point breaks any sense of monotony. A splendid example, too, of asymmetrical balance, in interesting contrast to the next reproduction.

Mrs. Ewing Philbin, Lawrence (L. I.) Garden Club
International Flower Show, New York
Class: Cut plant material in square or rectangular container.

achieved by the use of opposing primary hues rather than intermediate ones (see page *82*).

Split Complements. In the split complement, opposing hues are employed, but one of these is combined, not with its exact opposite but with hues on either side of that opposite. To take an example, yellow would be combined not with violet, but with blue and purple (see color circle page *89*). It is thus evident that in the split complement the principles of both opposition and analogy are united.

It is at once apparent that the split complement harmony will be a little more difficult to arrange and more subtle in its effect than the direct complement. The reader will find it interesting to compare the arrangement shown on page *147*, a fine example of a split complement harmony, in which purple is combined with yellow and green, to the more obvious direct harmony of orange and turquoise represented in the arrangement shown on page *105*.

In arrangements made for the home which must be "lived with" for a number of days, possibly a week, a split complement arrangement will often be found more satisfactory than a strong direct complement. It should be kept in mind, however, that the background and the container are factors to be considered quite as much as the flowers themselves, and their careful selection will go far toward subduing or toning down a direct complement composition which otherwise might be unpleasantly obvious or hard.

Triad Harmonies. In the triad harmony there is a combination of three hues equidistant from each other around the color circle. Red, blue and leaf (green) in the color circle shown on page *89* would constitute a triad harmony.

In the triad harmony, as the differences or distances between the hues employed are increased, the general effect resulting is more colorful. Triad color schemes are more likely to work out satisfactorily in arrangements in which a fairly large quantity of material is used. Otherwise a spotty effect is likely to result. This, however, is a general suggestion and by no means a fixed rule. Here again, too, the combination of primary colors will be much more dramatic than when intermediate hues are employed.

Tetrad Harmonies. The tetrad harmony is similar to the triad except that instead of three, four hues, each evenly spaced around the color circle, are joined in the combination. Thus yellow, jade, violet and red would constitute a tetrad harmony on the color circle shown on page *89*.

Tetrad harmonies are more difficult than any of the preceding to arrange successfully, since the danger of getting a spotty effect is increased. If carried out satisfactorily, tetrads are, of course, the most colorful of all. The greater the variety of plant material used and the larger the space occupied, the easier it will be to avoid failure. Whether the general effect be pleasing or distracting will depend very largely on how expert the arranger is in using shades, tints, or tones of the various hues that are in harmonizing value.

An excellent example of a tetrad in (approximately) red, yellow, jade, and a deep shade of violet is represented in the arrangement of fruits and flowers on page *151*.

VI

Color in Flower Arrangement

*J*UST AS WE FOUND that in building a pleasing design there were certain general principles to be followed, so in attempting to arrange a pleasing color harmony, there are certain things to strive for and others to avoid. Here our old friends, *composition*, *focus*, *balance* and *unity* bob up again in a new guise. They must be the guards standing at the gate to decide what shall be allowed to pass and what shall not. Composition says that there must be a pleasing pattern of color; balance that the several hues employed must be so distributed that because of size (area covered) or of intensity, any feeling of lopsidedness is avoided; focus, that the eye should be drawn to some central point; unity that no jarring or discordant note—not in keeping with the principles of harmony outlined in the preceding pages—shall creep in to mar the general effect that the flower artist is trying to create.

For an illustration of the practical application of these principles, it is suggested that the reader turn to the black and white reproduction of the arrangement on page *24* where it is evident that they have been employed successfully in the design, and then turn to the color reproduction of the same arrangement on page *37* where they apply with equal force to the *color scheme* used.

Setting the Key

Just as in a design in black and white, one line or combination of lines must dominate, so in attempting to establish any proposed color harmony, one key hue should be selected and the others made subservient to it. Otherwise a disquieting and annoying sense of strife is likely to result.

PLATE 25. *SYMPHONY IN ORANGE AND TURQUOISE*

*Here symmetrical balance in a pyramidal design has been combined with an
equally bold complementary color scheme. The background carries out the
desired feeling of Egyptian influence.*

Lady Gabriel, Bedford (N. Y.) Garden Club
International Flower Show, New York
Class: Cut plant material in any container to show Egyptian
    influence; 3rd prize.

It must be kept in mind, however, that cutting down the area allotted to a given hue is by no means the only method of controlling or subduing it. Hues of full intensity, such as those in the spectrum or the color circle, are much more dominating than their shades, tints, or tones.

In making a split complement harmony, then, the first color used, if it is somewhere near full intensity, easily dominates the two complementary colors employed with it if they are shades, tints, or tones even though the areas they occupy may be considerably greater. This is well illustrated in the arrangement on page *11*.

ACCENT BY CONTRAST

Frequently very dramatic effects can be secured by using a very small amount of a brilliant or vivid color placed in a strategic position which contrasts sharply with the hue or key color of the arrangement as a whole.

Turning once more to the coloration of a few familiar flowers we find that nature is adept at getting dramatic accents by this means. The brilliant golden beard of many blue irises, particularly among the bulbous type; the tiny thread of scarlet around the edge of the Poets' or Pheasant's Eye daffodil; the tiny golden eye of the African Violet and the green insignia at the tip of the inner petals of a Snowdrop are all familiar examples. Even among such pastel shades and tints as those of any of the flowers of the annual and hardy phloxes, the tiny contrasting eye gives them a peculiar charm.

It will be noted that in all these instances the position of the comparatively small spot of contrasting color has much to do with its effectiveness as an accent. Similarly in a flower arrangement, the position of such an accent is carefully chosen. Often it may be the focal point as in the arrangements on pages *131* and *237*.

Use of Black and White

In a certain technical sense black and white are not "colors," the former being the absence of all color (i.e. the absence of any reflected light waves that the human eye can register) and white being a combination of all hues. Psychologically, however, and in our everyday experiences, we recognize black and white as among the most important of colors. Gray, resulting from a mixture of black and white, is the third "hueless" color.

A gray made up of equal amounts of black and white is termed medium or neutral gray. It will be recalled that any pair of complementary colors opposite each other on the color circle when mixed in equal proportion also cancel into neutral gray.

Neutral gray, then, can be termed the lowest common denominator in our colors, including black and white. For this reason it is the most effective of all harmonizers. This is the basis for the assertion, frequently made, that any number of hues may be combined without disharmony if enough gray is used with them.

Of more importance to the arranger of flowers is the fact that shades, tints, and tones of any given hue harmonize not only with each other but also harmonize with other colors more readily than hues of full strength or value. This is the reason why so-called pastel colors blend or harmonize in almost any combination.

What has been said of the harmonizing qualities of tones (a full hue or color softened by the

PLATE 26. *STUDIED SIMPLICITY*

An excellent example of a symmetrical balance and of form harmony in container and plant material, the banana blossom and vase seeming made for each other. The sort of thing that looks easy—until it is tried!

Mrs. Gilbert Kinney, Greenwich (Conn.) Garden Club
International Flower Show, New York
Class: Flower picture. No restrictions, except proportion to space; 2nd prize.

addition of gray) applies also to shades and tints. It must be kept in mind, however, that what is gained in harmony in getting away from full strength hues is lost in vividness or dramatic quality. This loss can be compensated for by the use of a vivid note or highlight as already suggested.

The chief role played by black and white in flower arrangement is to strengthen other colors by contrast.

Just as gray tends to tone down or neutralize other colors in its vicinity so black and white tend to sharpen or heighten their effect by contrast. A single dark tulip (some of them such as La Tulipe Noire and Mystery are almost black) placed among white or lighter ones will make them appear still lighter. The reverse, of course, is equally true. Flowers of deep or dark tones, even though they do not begin to approach full black, heighten similarly those of light tint; and light colored flowers emphasize the quality of dark.

BACKGROUND AND LIGHTING

The experienced winner of show prizes in flower arrangement recognizes the very important role which backgrounds play. She either selects her own, or very carefully chooses her materials with regard to the backgrounds which may be supplied. With most amateurs interested chiefly in arranging flowers for home decoration, this important point is entirely overlooked. Even the most cursory survey of the color reproductions in this volume must make clear the fact that a well chosen background adds greatly to the general effect. One of the mistakes most commonly made and one which almost always can be avoided is that of placing the arrangement in front of a window or in some other position where the light is back of it. Even at many amateur flower shows this mistake is perpetrated.

Another common mistake is to place the arrangement in front of wallpaper or draperies with a conspicuous design, causing a visual confusion which kills any merit it may have.

It is well, too, to keep the arrangement at a fairly good distance in front of the background. Crowding too closely against it also results in confusion.

All of these suggestions are of a negative nature —things to avoid. What can be done to improve an arrangement by considering the effect of the background?

Desirable backgrounds are of three general types—neutral, harmonizing, and contrasting.

The object of a neutral background is to keep any disturbing element from entering into the picture. Being gray or grayish it not only stays out of the picture itself but serves the further purpose of helping to bring into harmony the colors used in the arrangement.

Harmonizing backgrounds may be selected in accordance with the principles already explained in connection with the flowers and the container. A background color which is analogous to or a complement of the key color of the arrangement will be selected. Examples of analogous backgrounds may be seen in the frontispiece and in the arrangement on page 203. Complementary backgrounds appear in the arrangements shown on pages 33 and 207.

Contrasting backgrounds, black and white, or light and dark, serve to throw the arrangement into bold relief thus making it both more dramatic and effective at a greater distance. Needless to say, to accomplish this purpose, a black or dark background will be used for a white or light colored arrangement, and vice versa.

HARMONY IN ACCESSORIES

The present trend in flower arrangement seems to be toward a freer and bolder use of accessories. In fact, in many recent examples they are so much an integral part of the whole arrangement that the term accessory really no longer applies. Examples of this trend appear in the frontispiece and in the color reproduction on page *105*. How far this new note in American flower arrangement is to be carried is yet to be determined, but it may very easily be overdone. Whatever happens so far as flower shows are concerned, those who are interested primarily in arrangements for home decoration should be chary of using accessories.

If accessories are used, their color relationship to plant material and container should be studied quite as carefully as that of any other part of the arrangement—possibly even more so because, with their semi-detached position and their difference from the plant material in shape and texture, they are doubly conspicuous. The color "tie up" between the accessories and plant material and container may be one of harmony by analogy or complement, or one of contrast. It should, however, not be too obvious—a mistake very frequently made. If an attempt is made to match some color in the arrangement, nothing short of a fairly perfect repetition of the original color should be acceptable. Any attempt along this line that does not quite "come off" is infinitely worse than none at all.

The amount of study which the average home owner, busy with a thousand and one other things, can devote to the intricacies of color harmony, is of course very limited. However the formation of the habit of self-criticism and a check up of such arrangements or "bouquets" as are made for home tables or mantlepieces will very soon result in worthwhile improvements in the color scheme involved.

The general principles of design and of color harmonies having been discussed, we will turn to the practical questions of handling our arrangements.

VII

Containers, Holders, and

Accessories

*A*s INTEREST GROWS in arranging flowers, the artist naturally begins to collect containers. The antique shop and auction rooms offer many possibilities, as do shops which sell modern glass and hand-made pottery. Oriental stores carry rare and beautiful containers of porcelain, bamboo, and bronze. The only limitations are those of the pocketbook and of available storage space.

Those who wish to limit their collections to a few pieces will do well to keep to neutral colors in which a great number of different flowers look well.

One large, open-necked jar or vase of wood, pottery, or metal is needed for long stemmed blooms which often come as gifts, or for such garden flowers as delphinium, stocks, and snap-dragons.

A large, low, open container, preferably oblong or oval, is the best thing to choose for Japanese line arrangements. White or gray-green are good color choices.

A medium-sized low bowl of pottery, brass, or copper will take care of many bulbous blooms and common garden flowers.

A round glass or porcelain bowl with a gener-ous opening is suitable for garden roses and other large headed blooms with stems of medium length.

An urn-shaped vase of classic design is useful for symmetrically arranged mass or semi-mass compositions.

Small jugs, pitchers, vases, and bowls can be chosen at will and in more decided colorings as these take up little room and are comparatively inexpensive.

Every flower artist has, or should have, a *pièce de résistance* or two for striking compositions. Perhaps these will include a beautiful blown glass

PLATE 27. *VEGETABLE STILL LIFE*

A whisk of scotch broom, a couple of kale leaves, a bunch of beets, and a hand-made container are all you need to win a blue ribbon—provided only they are properly put together. The "roses" carved from beets drew some criticism, but in this particular instance the end justified the means.

Mrs. Innis Brown, Douglaston (L. I.) Garden Club
International Flower Show, New York
Class: Scotch broom with other interesting material in a tall
dark container; 1st prize.

bottle, a Wedgewood jar or an ornately decorated "period" piece. The taste of the owner governs the selection, of course.

The woman who enters arrangement classes in flower shows must either own a large collection of containers or arrange to borrow what she needs from shops which are often glad to lend a few vases for such use.

If possible, it is helpful to have a cupboard or set of shelves for flower containers and holders near the counter and water faucets where arranging is done.

HOLDERS

Though the market is flooded with all sorts of gadgets for holding flower stems in place, only a very few holders are necessary to do a good job in arrangement.

Heavy metal holders which are divided into compartments and combined with plates of closely-set needle points on which to impale flower stems are perhaps the most efficient. These holders are substantial enough to hold rigid the branches of shrubs and heavy-stemmed flowers.

For bulbous blooms one can purchase sets of heavy lead tubes an inch or two in height which can be grouped to suit the plan of the arrangement.

Holders made of closely placed wire loops several inches high are effective for slim-stemmed garden flowers.

Tall wires with loops at the top, attached to a heavy lead base are excellent for arranging fragile vines and weak-stemmed flowers like petunias. The holder itself must be entirely concealed by stems and foliage.

Some holders of light weight metal are equipped with suction cups of rubber which fasten themselves firmly to the bottom of the container, thus holding the stems in exact position.

Many women like to buy strips of heavy sheet lead which can be bent and twisted at will to fit each arrangement made. With these it is often necessary to use stones or small rocks to conceal the holder and hold it firmly in place since it may be inclined to slip on a smooth surface.

Pebbles, gravel, and stones of moderate size— or cuttings from evergreen trees—can be packed inside a tall opaque container to hold stems in place.

In Japanese compositions, or line arrangements in low dishes, the holder can be successfully concealed by the use of interesting stones and bits of moss placed in a naturalistic manner.

Split twigs forced into the mouths of high-sided opaque containers of wood or unpolished metal in the Japanese manner will hold tall flower stems at the desired angle. These are not practical, however, for use in glazed pottery, porcelain, or polished metal.

ACCESSORIES

The flower artist who likes to create dramatic flower pictures either for display in her own home or for flower show competitions, will probably collect bits of miniature sculpture, carved jades, or crystals, and pottery and porcelain figurines to give emphasis to certain compositions.

The color, texture, period and spirit of such accessories must be carefully considered if they are to be successful.

A French arrangement in an urn or porcelain vase may be enhanced by the use of a miniature painted on ivory or a jeweled snuff box.

Victorian mass arrangements are often grouped with old fans, mother-of-pearl card cases, and the like.

Oriental line arrangements may be combined with a carving of old ivory or jade, a tiny sculptured Buddha (see reproduction page 3) or worshipfully gazing Oriental maiden, or even by a bronze toad.

Modern arrangements lend themselves to contemporary sculpture. Even abstractions in miniature fit the spirit of ultra-modern floral art.

Accessories, as their title indicates, do not draw attention too obviously from the arrangement itself but form an accompaniment that is harmonious but not emphatic.

At least, that has been the principle governing their use up to now. Several distinguished prize winners at the 1940 International Flower Show struck out boldly by giving equal importance to flowers and supplementary material. In two instances, at least, these arrangements were so successful as to form precedents which may be followed hereafter.

One of these groupings—appropriate to the war year 1940—showed a spirited carving in wood of three youthful poilus marching arm in arm to some unheard marching tune. Behind them and to their right a tall, straight-sided glass jar held a sheaf of fleur-de-lis. The carving, full of character and interest, was perhaps six or seven inches high and—since it depicted three figures marching abreast—was of considerable width. It was too emphatic to be considered an accessory. In fact it was *the* focal point of the grouping, and the flowers stepped into the background, completing the theme but subservient to the blue-clad, alert figures with their air of heart-rending youthful bravado.

The other prize winner used a brilliantly colored procelain figure of considerable height in the foreground of the composition. As the reader may expect, the figure was, to say the least, of equal importance with the arrangement of flowers which it complemented.

Both these arrangements were so arresting, so satisfying to the eye, and stimulating to the imagination that the writers feel they may strike a new and revolutionary note in the use of so-called "accessories."

VIII

Cutting and Caring for Plant

Material

𝓕EW ARRANGEMENTS ARE long lasting unless the plant material has been "hardened" before it is placed in the container.

Garden flowers picked very early in the morning—or if that is impossible, after the sun goes down at night—should be placed in deep receptacles filled with cool water in a cellar or dark cool closet for several hours, or over night. This process prepares the blooms for handling and display at room temperature.

Overnight hardening is recommended for peonies, gladiolus, iris, all large stemmed blooms.

In cutting garden flowers, select only buds and freshly opened blooms which will stand the shock of cutting and which have their full blooming period before them. Carry a pail of water into the garden and carefully place each flower in this as soon as it is cut, keeping varieties separate, and stems and foliage disentangled. By this means the shock of cutting is greatly lessened, and the flowers begin to recover promptly or even fail to droop at all.

Cut each stem cleanly at an angle with a sharp knife or flower cutter. The angular cut prevents the stems from adhering closely to the bottom of the water receptacle, and they are thus able to absorb more water.

Woody-stemmed flowers such as chrysanthemums and flowering shrubs absorb water better if their stems are crushed for several inches at the base.

Poppies, poinsettias, and other blooms with milky juices, keep much better if the tips of the stems are seared in a flame as soon as they are cut.

Dahlias, gerberas, heliotrope, and all flowers with hollow stems should have the stem tips dipped in boiling water.

PLATE 28. *UNUSUAL COLOR*

Here line and mass have been combined in a design of great originality, and a wide color range has skillfully been kept in harmony. The repetition of the green and white of the pandanus foliage in the two ivy leaves at the base is a skillful touch.

Mrs. Stephen McClelland
Judges' Course of the Federated Garden Clubs of New York State
Class: Composition of foliage stressing line, using fruit for
   accent; 2nd prize.

Care must be taken that the steam or flame does not affect blooms or foliage.

When arranging flowers, remove all foliage which would be under water. If retained, this decays and causes the flowers to deteriorate quickly.

Tiny phials which hold a few drops of water keep boutonnieres fresh for many hours. Orchids placed in a humidifier in the refrigerator between wearings will last a long time in good condition.

There are several chemicals now available commercially which are intended to lengthen the life of cut flowers. Like the exploded theory of adding aspirin or salt, some of these preservatives do not give convincing results. Others, tested by authorities, are really effective. "Flora-life" is one which has produced good results.

Purchasing Flowers

When purchasing flowers, it is always well to buy direct from a grower or wholesaler if possible. If a retail shop is chosen, talk your problem over with the proprietor and arrange to get only freshly delivered material. It is cheaper in the end.

PLATE 29. *STUDY IN BLUE AND GREEN*

An out-of-the-ordinary vertical arrangement, in which the use of a flaring base preserves the feeling of stability and keeps the material from looking top-heavy in the vase. Texture tie-up with the container is good.

Mrs. Frederick W. Lewis, Little Neck (L. I.) Garden Club
Judges' Course of the Federated Garden Clubs of New York State
Class: Composition of foliage stressing line, using fruit for
accent; 1st prize and Tricolor.

Flowers sold along the roadside or in open markets may not last until they reach home. If buying such cut material, try to get blooms which have been cut and set away to harden in a dark place. Sunshine, wind, handling, and insufficient water play havoc even with field-grown flowers.

If many hours must elapse between purchase and display, keep the material in a cool place in deep water or, if the blooms must be "held back," under low refrigeration.

In selecting flowers at a shop do not deceive yourself into believing that soft "floppy" blossoms or foliage will "come back," that gardenias which are off-white are fresh, or that chrysanthemums which drop a petal or have discolored petals at the back of the flower are fit to buy.

IX

Plant Material for Arrangements Throughout The Year

SPRING

THIS IS THE SEASON when all Nature is offering us material for arrangements. With such a wealth to choose from, the natural inclination is to mass great jars or vases full of daffodils, tulips, fruit blossoms, flowering shrubs, and a score of other favorites. But for distinctive compositions of good design which show blossoms, foliage shapes, and branch forms to the best advantage, it is often wise to use plant material sparingly, no matter how plentiful it may be.

As this is written, thousands of daffodils of almost a hundred varieties, running the color gamut from pure white to deepest orange and apricot are in bloom in the garden. Fruit trees and shrubs are in full flower also. I could have tubs and jars filled to overflowing with the bloom from my own acres. But that sort of wholesale cutting and massing does not give accent to any blossom or branch of tender leaves and buds.

Beside me in an open dish are three branches of apple, the pink buds just bursting open. Their graceful curves and the silhouette made by each leaf and cluster of blossoms makes this line grouping a thing of beauty which gives pleasure in the same way that a fine etching, print, or painting gladdens the eye. The bits of porous rock gathered near an old smelter, which support the base and conceal the flower holder lend color contrast and interesting texture to the composition.

A tall vase on a hall table contains five great white-petaled *Incomparabilis* daffodils and a few sprays of flowering almond in tight bud. Like five huge white pearls set with smaller precious stones, this arrangement has a rare, jewel-like perfection. Five tiny, nodding white *Triandrus*

PLATE 30. *ALTAR-FLAME*

Extreme modernism is represented in this dramatic geometric design in which the glass vase repeats the triangular motif. The altar-flame effect of the red leaf at the focal point is especially good. Symmetrical balance, focus, and unity are all well exemplified here.

Mrs. Edward C. Blum, South Side (L. I.) Garden Club
International Flower Show, New York
Class: Cut plant material in an American Glass container of any
    period; 1st prize.

hybrids grace a blue pottery dish on the breakfast table.

With a total of a dozen or two blossoms and a handful of blooming branches, the house is decked with spring and yet the compositions used are an integral part of the interior decoration. There is no sense of funereal or bridal opulence.

Daffodils and tulips are of course the two main groups of spring flowering bulbs available for cut flower arrangement. Today the great number of varieties of both makes it easy for the flower artist to find colors, sizes, and forms to suit her containers.

Daffodils. Daffodils are tall, medium, and short; early, mid-season, and late; as big as butter plates, or as small as a nickel. The colors vary from pure, virginal white, through cream to primrose, lemon yellow, gold, orange, pink, apricot, and oxblood red. There are yellow trumpets of all sizes; white trumpets; bi-colors with the trumpets a shade deeper than the perianth or outer petals; pink or apricot trumpets surrounded by cream white perianths. Other sorts have fluted or ruffled shorter cups of orange, yellow or cream, or yellow edged or shading into orange. And there are the pheasant's-eyes with broad white perianths and flat cups edged with red. The *poetaz* hybrids bear several small scented blooms on a stem. Tiny rock garden varieties and species in white, yellow, or orange are little taller than snowdrops, while such towering giants as Alcida and Nobility are four inches in diameter on great stalwart stems, with broad blue-green foliage.

Varieties especially recommended for arrangement are: the Jonquil hybrids, Chrysolite, tall yellow; Golden Sceptre, yellow; Buttercup and Tullus Hostillius, small yellow; Odorus Orange Queen, a tiny orange; La Vestale, white trumpet; Gertie Millar, a lovely *Leedsii* with white perianth and primrose cup; John Evelyn, an *Incomparabilis*, with broad, white perianth, four to five inches across and a densely frilled flat cup of pure lemon yellow; Francisca Drake, another *Incomparabilis* with a white perianth with a yellow cup shading to deepest orange. Among the dainty, flat-cupped, fairy-like varieties are Sunrise, a star-shaped, smallish flower with a white perianth stained orange yellow near the base and a dainty orange yellow cup; Hera, which is all pure white when mature; and Queen of the North, white and yellow. *Triandrus* hybrids, Agnes Harvey and Moonshine, are pure white, rock garden fairies.

Tulips. Like daffodils, tulips offer infinite variety in size, color, form, and season of bloom. They begin with the Spring-flowering Earlies, double and single, medium sized, colorful blossoms, some as double as a peony, others chaste in their single perfection. The new tall Triumph class is early also, followed by the medium sized Cottage Tulips and the Parrots, with their colorful, ragged petals, marked with pale green along the mid-vein on the outer side. These are indicated for bold, striking compositions in the modern spirit. Later in the season come the Lily-flowered varieties, which are particularly excellent for arrangements, and the huge, stiff but brilliant Darwins and majestic, darkly rich Breeders. These two last mentioned types are suitable chiefly for formal compositions, carefully thought out and executed. (See page *61*.) The tiny Botanical or Species tulips are unexcelled for small groupings. Except for the brilliant scarlet Eichleri and Red Emperor with its bizarre black center, most of these are delicately colored.

PLATE 31. *WHY "RULES" ARE NOT SAFE*

A first glance at this charming modern mass arrangement might indicate that the use of heavy broad foliage with small and rather light and airy blossoms violates the principle of unity. But the foliage has been so placed as to seem part of the vase rather than of the cut flower material.

Mrs. Magnus Norstad, Valhalla (N. Y.) Garden Club
International Flower Show, New York
Class: Cut plant material in suitable container against a yellow-
   green background. No accessories; 2nd prize.

Varieties recommended for arrangement are:

Double earlies. Peachblossom, rose pink; Tea-rose; Schoonoord, white; and Marechal Niel, soft canary flushed with orange.

Single earlies. DeWet, light orange scarlet, delightfully fragrant for indoor use; La Reve, soft rose and buff.

Lily-Flowering. White Cross, with petals which appear crinkled, pure white but suffused with yellow before maturity; Mrs. Moon, yellow; Sirene, rose and white, with wavy, reflexed petals.

Parrots. Gadelan, orchid-like in shape and color; Fantasy, pink, with laciniated petals.

Darwins. La Tulipe Noire, blackish maroon; La France, rose pink; Afterglow, rose and salmon; Duke of Wellington, white.

Breeders. Copernicus, coppery-bronze with a rosy bloom; Indian Chief, Indian brown and copper; Rayon D'Or, golden bronze; Roi Soleil, violet blue and bronze.

Botanicals. Kaufmanniana, the Water-lily Tulip, 12 inches high, creamy yellow marked with bright carmine; Clusiana, delicate elongated blooms, white and rose red; Eichleri, crimson and black.

PLATE 32. *FIRE AND WATER*

A bold strong touch in the use of color contrasts is characteristic of most arrangements in the modern manner. Here subtle harmonies and repetitions have been added to supplement the contrasts.

Mrs. Frederick W. Lewis, Little Neck (L. I.) Garden Club
International Flower Show, New York
Class: Invitation—Modern still life. Flower arrangement required; special award.

Minor Bulbs. Blooming snowdrops, grape hyacinths, *chionodoxas*, lilies-of-the-valley, crocuses and other minor bulbs can be dug up, roots and all, for use in "living plant arrangements" indoors in spring. These may be combined with periwinkle, ivy or other vines, moss, stones, and suitable supplementary material.

Wildlings. Such tiny wildlings as marsh marigolds, violets, bloodroot, arbutus, spring beauties, and fringed polygala may be lifted, roots and all, from their garden beds for a few days very early in spring to grace a wide, low dish indoors. Banked with moss and rocks and arranged naturalistically, these are a constant delight in a living room, dining room, or sun porch. A taller branch of blooming swamp maple, benzoine, or shadbush gives the effect of a sapling towering above the wildflowers. When bloom is over, the rooted plants go back to their homes in the garden beds, where they readily re-establish themselves.

Miniatures of myosotis, violas, tiny Plumy Bleedingheart, and other early spring blooms are heartening on the breakfast tray or in the sick room.

Flowering Shrubs. The common spring-flowering shrubs, tamarisk, *philadelphus*, lilac, *Cydonia japonica*, viburnum, pussywillow, forsythia, flowering almond, spice-bush, and what have you, are splendid supplementary material for cut flower arrangements. Graceful, curving branches without awkward angles are selected to give height and rhythmic curves. The magnolias make distinguished and "important" line arrangements although they are a bit difficult to handle.

LATE SPRING AND EARLY SUMMER

As the late spring and early summer flowers arrive there are endless possibilities for indoor decoration.

Among the daintier flowers are bleedingheart with its unusual blossoms and foliage, and columbine, that delicate bloom which looks like a flight of winged jewels. Both these are "naturals" for line arrangement, with their distinctive shapes and beautiful foliage which stand out so well in silhouette. Narrow-necked glass bottles of interesting design are often used for these flowers.

Peonies. These come around Memorial Day in the Northeast and are heavy headed and difficult to arrange in mass. One, two, or three blooms, however, cut short, and with buds and their distinctive foliage can be made into showy and interesting line or modified line arrangements. Tree peonies, if available, are especially good because of their characterful branches and foliage. Some of the lovely single varieties are also preferable to the usual, cabbage-like doubles.

Iris. The Japanese arrange Iris with artful and sparing simplicity. It is graceful grouped alone with its own foliage in low containers, or combined with other flowers in mass or semi-mass compositions. Though some of the new Tall Bearded varieties are delightful in color, form, and habit of growth, they are often almost too big for use as cut flowers. Others of medium size are preferable.

The rock garden varieties, dwarf and semi-dwarf, can however be made use of as well as the graceful Siberians with their fine foliage, the orchid-like bulbous varieties (see page 53) and the exotic Japanese. Most of the American species and species hybrids, especially *Fulva* and its

PLATE 33. *PERFECT BALANCE*

*With a container of this type (suggestive of a wheel) the greatest skill is
required to achieve perfect balance—in this instance so well done that it
matches the poise of a Japanese tight-wire walker.*

Mrs. Frederick W. Lewis, Little Neck (L. I.) Garden Club
Judges' Course of the Federated Garden Clubs of New York State
Class: Modern composition.

[141]

various sub-types, and hybrids, such as Dorothy K. Williamson, make unusual material for arrangements and have the advantage of flowering between the Tall Bearded and the Japanese.

Broad-leaved Evergreens. At this season, too, broad-leaved evergreens and some deciduous flowering shrubs are in bloom. Azaleas, both wild and hybridized, start the show, giving white, pink, rose, cerise, salmon, and orange blossoms. Leucothoë, and pieris with their graceful drooping bells, are followed by laurel and rhododendron.

The lovely glossy foliage of these broad-leaved evergreens are valuable supplementary material in flower arrangement the year round. (See color reproductions on pages *41, 65, 71, 75,* and *183.*) while the showy flowers make unique compositions at blooming time. Blooms and foliage, even from valuable shrubs, may usually be carefully pruned without injuring the shape or condition of the plant. Such cuttings are ideal for use as the focal center of a composition or for a "one flower" Japanese arrangement. A cluster of rhododendron florets surrounded by its paddle-wheel of glossy leaves is effective for a composition in the modern manner. The drooping bells of leucothoë or pieris together with the glossy foliage can be combined with more colorful flowers. Laurel, though so lovely in itself, is not easy to arrange, but a fine cluster of bloom with foliage can be used as a focal center with supplementary material.

Roses. These flowers, which come first in June, are difficult to arrange skillfully, but always worth the trouble because of their perfection and fragrance. Sprays of climbing or trailing varieties, as well as the cluster-flowered Polyanthas and larger-flowered Floribundas, lend themselves to treatment in wall vases, hanging baskets, or mantel vases, low and open mouthed.

The great hybrid teas and perpetuals are traditionally placed in crystal or silver bowls though there are many more original ways of arranging them. (See pages *13* and *53*.) These two illustrations, the first a mass composition, the second a delicate line grouping, show the latitude possible in arranging roses. Roses—especially florists' roses with their straight stems—have since time immemorial been massed together without supplementary material, but this outworn custom gives little opportunity to enjoy the individual blossoms or leaf patterns. Garden roses which grow more gracefully than those commercially produced are easier to arrange either in a line or a modified mass grouping. Combined with fuchsias, passionflower vines or—as old-fashioned fragrant bouquets in tuzzy-muzzy vases—with mignonette, lavender, and lemon verbena, they have a charm all their own.

Poppies. These flowers which are often considered too fragile and fleeting for use in arrangements can have their lives prolonged by the treatment recommended in Chapter VI. On page *95* we have an example of their possibilities, while page *33* shows a superb grouping of ranunculus, another flower generally thought too frail for cutting.

Midsummer

Gladiolus. The gladiolus continues to be a first rate florists' flower because of its showy and varied colors, lovely form and texture, and long-lasting qualities. More unsightly vases of it have probably been arranged, however, than of any

PLATE 34. *EFFECTIVE BACKGROUND*

This subdued but rich arrangement—in which the repetition of the color of the Tokay grapes, provided by the pineapple flower bud, is a very clever touch—is made doubly effective by the background used.

Mrs. Ralph V. Magoffin, Associated Member of the Federated Garden Clubs of New York State
International Flower Show, New York
Class: Pedestal arrangement of tropical foliage, fruit on branches or stems permitted, tall dark container requested; 1st prize.

other flower. The straight spikes of brilliant color are usually present in ornate florists' baskets, hotel lobby jars, and funeral pieces.

By consulting page *57* one can study what is being done with gladiolus by intelligent and imaginative artists. Here again the exercise of restraint in the use of material results in a much more distinguished composition than that shown on page *201*, where the spikes have been placed to display a number of superb specimen blooms.

The smaller-flowered and more graceful *primulinus* varieties and hybrids are easier to arrange. Brightsides is a gay member of this informal group. For a large, stately spike, nothing could be lovelier than the shell-like perfection of the new and justly famous Greta Garbo.

Summer Flowering Bulbs. The other summer flowering bulbs, tigridia, ismene, Cape hyacinth and montbretia provide material for unusual and striking compositions in cut flowers. They should be grown more generally than they are.

Garden Lilies. These graceful and distinctive flowers can be placed in tall containers in an arrangement similar to that used for the Easter lilies shown on page *49*, using buds, half-opened,

PLATE 35. *EFFECTIVE SIMPLICITY*

The remarkably perfect harmony, in both texture and color, of base and container lend interest to this solution of the difficult problem of making an arrangement that may be viewed from any angle—a problem often not successfully solved in table arrangements.

Mrs. James Hathaway, Pelham Manor (N. Y.) Garden Club
Judges' Course of the Federated Garden Clubs of New York State
Class: An arrangement to be viewed from any side; 1st prize.

[147]

and full blown flowers, and supplementary material; or they make delicately colored and characterful table arrangements if the stems are cut and the blooms placed in low dishes of silver, crystal, or fine, highly glazed pottery which blends with the texture of the blooms.

The smaller or "Pygmy" waterlilies, (such as Yellow Pygmy and White Pygmy and Patricia) also in bloom in midsummer, are especially good for the center of the luncheon table. They are most effective floating on the surface of a large dish of open water with their own leaves and a bit of rock or lump of crystal to support them in position.

Other Garden Flowers. Moonflowers, cut at dusk, will remain open through dinner and until early next morning. Their delicious fragrance as well as their exotic beauty of form and texture recommends them for table arrangements. A vine bearing several blooms and some foliage is effective arranged in one of the circular or oval table containers with a hollow center designed for massing chopped-off flowerheads in close rows to give a formal, geometric pattern of color. Though we do not approve of the sort of "arrangement"—if it may be called that—for which these dishes were made, they are lovely holding vines, violas, violets, myosotis, or tiny primulas, foliage and all.

For the mixed, informal bouquets of mid-summer which stand on porches, terraces, and in living rooms, it is fun to mix practically everything, thus getting a riot of color at a colorful season. The spikes of snapdragon blend admirably with calendulas, early dwarf dahlias, zinnias, and salpiglossis.

Petunias are effective arranged alone, in bowls or dishes which show off the individual flowers and interesting, bent stems. They are not easy to do well, though the single varieties behave better when cut than do the large flowered Fluffy Ruffles type. A special holder is helpful with tall wires for support which are hidden by the foliage.

Nasturtiums, marigolds, shasta daisies, gaillardias and scabiosas are but a few of the summer blooms which look well anywhere, arranged unconventionally in pottery or metal bowls and dishes, or in stone jars, or colorful pitchers. Even such fantastic blooms as tritomas are remarkably distinctive in a line arrangement; while cosmos, verbenas, asters, salpiglossis, blue lace-flower, anchusa and all the daintier annuals and perennials can be used for table, bed room, and dainty summer living room compositions of an informal type.

Autumn

In autumn most of the midsummer flowers continue until frost and to these are added delicate, beautifully formed anemones, the showy dahlias, large and small, the riot of hardy chrysanthemums, and daisy-like hardy asters.

Dahlias. Large flowered dahlias are not good subjects for arrangement usually, though an arrangement such as that on page *209* proves that there is an exception to every rule. But the colorful little Unwin Dwarfs, Coltness Hybrids and Orchid-flowered types, which bloom right through from late summer to frost, offer a great variety of color and form to the flower artist. There are a number of warm gold and salmon pink combinations in the doubles which make good focal interest where spikes of rose and gold snapdragons are used for height. The deep

PLATE 36. *GRECIAN INFLUENCE*

Unity, simplicity, and symmetrical balance, typical characteristics of Grecian art and architecture, are well portrayed in the spirit of this rather massive composition done in the modern manner.

Mrs. Thomas H. Blodgett, Lenox (Mass.) Garden Club
International Flower Show, New York
Class: Cut plant material in any container to show Grecian influence; 2nd prize.

scarlets, crimsons, and garnets sometimes have beautiful dark foliage. Or they can be combined with autumn leaves, fruited barberry, or the foliage of variegated house plants. Whites, clear yellows, golds, and pinks are also plentiful. Another small flowered but taller-growing dahlia of great distinction is Bishop of Llandaff, with its rich dark reddish foliage. Mt. Everest, Newport Wonder, Dahliadel Twinkle, and Snow White are but a few of a score or more more small flowered sorts which are lovely in arrangements.

Chrysanthemums. Korean hybrid chrysanthemums are beautiful in mass arrangements because their many colors blend so softly and pleasantly. The larger flowered sorts make effective line compositions. (See pages *91* and *225*.)

In this wonderful new hybrid type there are many varieties to choose from. Pygmy Gold and Urchin are two small-flowered varieties with pompom blood in them. Rose Glow is larger, double, and a beautiful warm color. Lavender Lady and Pale Moon are large, light colored doubles which are lovely in combination. The Moor, Burgundy, and Autumn Tints are darker and richer, with a golden sheen on the reverse side of the petals. All are worth growing and desirable for cutting.

Among the florists' chrysanthemums are the large-flowered clustered and ragged-petaled single types, the anemone-flowered and other distinctive forms which lend character to an arrangement, as a glance at page *217* will show. The huge cabbage-headed straight-stemmed "exhibition" sorts are difficult for indoor decoration.

WINTER

Florists' Flowers. Those who can afford to buy flowers for winter decoration have ample material to choose from. Exotic gardenias and camelias (page *231*); rare and interesting orchids (frontispiece and page *29*); the strange and colorful strelitzia (page *131*), together with anthuriums, are but a few of the more interesting materials. Calla lilies are very effective when combined with variegated caladium leaves or other supplementary material, as illustrated in the. arrangements on pages *57* and *233*. Fruits are colorful and interesting and can be used with ingenuity. (See pages *125* and *151*.)

[153]

Forced Bulbs. The best source of supply in winter for the person of moderate means is to be found in home-forced bulbs, both tender and spring-flowering. Freesias, callas, amaryllis, clivia, and crinum are among the most satisfactory of the former. For amaryllis arrangements see pages *21* and *137*. Page *105* demonstrates a novel use of clivia blossoms. The daintier freezias are effective in arrangements showing French influence or in a sophisticated line composition.

Forced spring-flowering bulbs make it possible to bring spring indoors months ahead of time. Most of the early daffodils force successfully as well as the Single and Double Early Tulips. Wm. Copeland, Fred Moore, Gen. DeWet, La Reve, Sirene, Fantasy, and Gemma are all good forcing tulips. Crocuses and other minor spring bulbs also force very well.

House Plant Foliage. For supplementary material in arrangements and occasionally for the whole composition, the foliage of houseplants is unexcelled. Leaves of aspidistra, dieffenbachia, pandanus, philodendron (page *125*), fiddle-leaved rubber plant (page *155*), cryptanthus (page *29*),

PLATE 37. *MONOCHROME*

*This delightful modern arrangement made with dried material well illus-
trates the fact that pleasing compositions may be achieved without bright
colors. One great advantage of dry material arrangements is that they may
be enjoyed for weeks or months.*

Mrs. Magnus Norstad, Valhalla (N. Y.) Garden Club
International Flower Show, New York
Class: Invitation—Still life in browns and grays using dried
materials. One other color if desired; special award.

sedums (page *147*), monstera (page *37*) and lo-
quat (page *237*) are but a few of these which are
now used widely in arrangements of distinction.

Dried Material. Seed pods, dried grasses, and
fruits are still popular for winter arrangement,
and the artist who is interested in this sort of
composition can comb the autumn countryside to
good purpose. Pages *155*, *159*, *163*, and *167* show
good examples of dried material groupings.
Shells, corals, and other under-sea material, such
as is used in the arrangement on page *161* may be
employed for another form of winter arrangement which is long-lasting, unusual, and interesting.

Evergreen Branches. The branches of coniferous
evergreens as well as the foliage of the broad-
leaved types are beautiful in form and coloring.
Sometimes a single bloom is all that is needed for
emphasis, as in the arrangement on page *11*.

Forced Flowering Shrubs. As spring approaches,
forced spring-flowering shrubs keep the house
gay from February to April. Most people force
forsythia but seldom think to try other shrubs,
many of which bloom indoors equally well.

X

Do's and Don'ts for Beginners

*E*XPERIENCED arrangers know instinctively what to do and what not to do in building up a floral composition. Those who are learning, however, often make obvious mistakes which can be easily remedied if one learns to see them before the design is completed.

It is interesting to visit the annual flower shows of a new club for several consecutive years. The general average of excellence rises by leaps and bounds, showing that the decisions of the judges each year teach exhibitors why some failed and others won.

DO'S

Among the obvious *"Do's"* for beginners, whether they are arranging flowers for the home or for flower show competitions are:

1. Use only material which is in good condition. Overblown or faded flowers do not pay for the time spent in arranging them.

2. Have plant material well hardened in advance. (See page *124.*)

3. Select a container which holds enough water to keep the material alive. An inch of water in an open dish won't suffice through the dinner hour for a group of thirsty, thick-stemmed tulips or daffodils.

4. Unless you have exactly the right container for an arrangement—the perfect complement for the plant material—use a conservative, unobtrusive receptacle which cannot detract from the arrangement even though it cannot add much to it.

5. When using a conspicuously colored or shaped, or ornately decorated, container, start with that and select flowers and foliage to go with it.

PLATE 38. *BURRS AND SEED PODS*

*A circular design made with materials most beginners would be likely to
ignore. The carefully chosen background and accessory carry out the monochrome harmony and give additional interest.*

Mrs. William Hutchinson, Garden City-Hempstead (L. I.) Community Club
International Flower Show, New York
Class: Invitation—Still life in browns and grays using dried
materials. One other color if desired; special award.

6. See to it that you have and use efficient flower holders which will not let you—and the flower stems—down.

7. Make yourself comfortable at a wide counter or table with newspapers on which to clip stems and discarded foliage; good shears or cutters, and water nearby.

8. Take plenty of time and enjoy yourself as you would if you were sketching or doing other creative work.

9. When the composition is nearly finished, check it for faults in composition, focal interest, balance and unity. (See chapter II.)

10. When the result is satisfactory, place the arrangement and leave it alone. Don't try to gild the lily.

DON'TS

The "*Don'ts*" are, if possible, even more important to the beginner. So don't:

1. Leave an open space near the middle of the composition which looks as though a heavy shot had plowed through it. The eye seeks this and it becomes the focal point.

PLATE 39. *FOR A MERMAID'S BOUDOIR*

Marine specimens arranged without a container, thus providing a more
natural effect. Though the design is a bit oversize for the space, this is
largely offset by the filmy character of the materials.

Mrs. William Meissner, Garden City-Hempstead (L. I.) Community Club
International Flower Show, New York
Class: Invitation—Still life in browns and grays using dried
   materials   One other color if desired; special award.

2. Use asparagus fern or gypsophilla to fill in open spaces. Select foliage which is interesting in form, color, or both.

3. Fill in the open space about the base of the arrangement with a wreath of short-stemmed flowers or severed leaves. The result is artificial and distracting to the eye.

4. Think it necessary to use every scrap of material in the florist's box or garden pail in one arrangement.

5. Crowd your material so that stems cross each other, one blossom hides another, or foliage is bunched together like spinach.

6. Copy other peoples' masterpieces in different colors and materials. Someone may catch you at it.

7. Watch your neighbor in a competition and try to incorporate in your arrangement some of the features of hers. Concentrate on your own inspiration.

8. Be afraid to use a common garden weed, vegetable foliage, or any unconventional material. The unusual helps give originality to a composition if cleverly arranged.

PLATE 40. *EGYPT*

In this striking composition the pyramidal "accessory" becomes part of the background and strikes the keynote for the whole design. The modeling of the base cloth to give an effect of desert sands is a clever touch.

Mrs. Edward Emerson, Hortulus Club, Greenwich, Connecticut
International Flower Show, New York
Class: Cut plant material in any container to show Egyptian
  influence; 2nd prize.

9. Fail to use the clippers on unneeded foliage or branching stems.

10. Leave a confusion of books, nicknacks, or other impedimenta on the table near a lovely arrangement. Let it stand alone on its merits, well lighted, and with a suitable background.

XI

Japanese Arrangements

THE MUCH DISCUSSED and much studied subject of Japanese floral art is too complicated to be covered fully in a book on American flower arrangement. A brief consideration of the history and modern progress of this important phase of flower decoration will help, however, to clarify some of its more perplexing mysteries.

So-called "Japanese Flower Art" has been a part of that country's religious and social tradition since the Sixth Century, when a Japanese emissary to China brought back to his native land a custom of the Chinese Buddhist priests—that of placing formally arranged groups of cut flowers on the temple altars.

This early beginning constituted the first "school" of Japanese flower art, and from it have sprung all the others. Perhaps it is because of the religious significance in Oriental flower arrangements that masters have disagreed from time to time, younger devotees splitting off from their parent school to form new schools of their own, each with its own set of hidebound rules and taboos, but each maintaining many of the original principles. In short, the history of Japanese flower art is not unlike that of the Christian religion, with its many sects and frequent "splits."

Each master artist, however, whose gift has been sufficiently distinguished for it to be perpetuated as a distinct school, has made some contribution of a constructive sort to the ever growing snowball of this conventionalized Japanese art. For many centuries now, flower arrangement has been not only an expression of religious feeling but an integral part of the secular culture and social expression of the Japanese people.

It is interesting also to note that just as we in the West have been influenced by the East, so

PLATE 41. *"ATMOSPHERE"*

Subtle suggestions of the hooded cobra of the Cairo snake charmer, the lotus of the Nile, and (in the container) oriental water jars give this dramatic arrangement unusual "unity of atmosphere."

Mrs. John R. Delafield, Millbrook (L. I.) Garden Club
International Flower Show, New York
Class: Cut plant material in any container to show Egyptian influence; 1st prize.

modern Japanese flower artists have learned something from us and are producing compositions of a freer, less formalized style than was formerly used.

For the purposes of this book it is sufficient to say that the many schools of Japanese flower arrangement are divided into two general camps: the strictly formal and conventional, and the free, imaginative, and naturalistic. A few of these styles are discussed further later on in this chapter.

Though the rules and conventions differ widely in the many schools which have developed in Japan and though there is a variation in the very terms used to designate the elements of the floral compositions in these schools, all retain the same chief principles of design—the simple yet vital requirements which have made Japanese floral art such an important influence in the development of flower arrangement here in America.

JAPANESE PRINCIPLES OF ARRANGEMENT

Japanese flower arrangements, whether they belong to the *Ikenobo*, *Ikebana*, or *Nageire* school—

to mention but three of the many—are invariably built on a triangular skeleton. Though there may be five, seven, nine, or any other odd number of flowers or plant stems in a grouping, the three main lines of the arrangement—the supports on which the composition is built—are always dominant. In Japanese arrangement *line*, not mass, is the important thing. Every stem, bud, leaf, and twig is made to do its work—to stand out as a part of the silhouette which makes the design.

Of the three main lines which form the skeleton:

A, the longest line (known in Japan as the "Heaven" line) is arbitrarily ruled to be one and one-half times the height of any tall vase containing it, or one and one-half times the diameter of any shallow dish.

B, the secondary line (called in Japan the "Man" line) is two-thirds the length of line A.

c, the tertiary line (named by Japanese the "Earth" line) is one-third the length of A.

By referring to the diagrams on pages *176* and *177*, it is evident that any arrangement built on these proportions must have a triangular pattern. Though the rules governing the length of these

three main lines may appear arbitrary to the un-
initiated, the principles of design are such that
experiment will prove the essential rightness of
their proportions.

With lines A, B, and c to build with, all sorts
of triangular line arrangements can be arrived at,
and each will be graceful and well balanced.

In adding more plant material to a Japanese arrangement, the three main lines are never over-
shadowed or confused. They always remain
dominant and clear cut.

The tips of all branches or flower sprays point
upward "in an aspiring manner" as though the
material were growing and reaching toward the
light.

Branches which cross each other are considered
bad form because these cross lines confuse the
design and distract the eye; and two or more
flowers are never placed at the same level in a
composition because this creates an effect of
"stepping" which is monotonous and unpleasing.

Flowers or blossoms which hang down on the
under side of a main line are always removed,
though foliage may remain if it does not interfere
with the free flow of the curve.

PLATE 42. *TRIANGLE*

*In this green and tan composition the dried okra pods give a strong sil-
houette that carries out the triangular design while avoiding a too solid
mass. (Okra, incidentally, has lovely flowers, as well as being an in-
gredient of famous southern soups, and is easily grown anywhere.)*

Mrs. Joseph Gazzam, Larchmont (N. Y.) Garden Club
Judges' Course of the Federated Garden Clubs of New York State
Class: Arrangement of dried material; 1st prize.

Following the general principles of good design which are alike the world over, the Japanese place dark colored and full-blown flowers low in the composition, with buds and half-opened blooms higher in the grouping.

SYMBOLISM

Because Oriental flower art is full of the religious and social symbolism which delights the Eastern mind, the three lines A, B, and C are called respectively the lines of Heaven, Man, and Earth; the tallest vertical line representing aspiration toward the immortal; while the second line symbolizes man himself; and the third, or shortest line, the earth on which he spends his mortal life.

Since there is symbolic significance to every flower, leaf, stone, and bit of bark used in a Japanese arrangement, plant materials and accessories are selected with meticulous care. Thus black stones are used in winter and light colored ones in summer. Winter arrangements show little water, but summer groupings have a cool and spacious effect produced by the use of open con-

tainers showing comparatively large water areas or tall jars filled to the brim. Since an interpretation of Nature is always striven for, plant materials are always of a type which may be found growing together, and hot house blooms are considered artificial and in bad taste.

Buds, occupying positions of importance high in arrangements, symbolize the future, full-blown blossoms the present, and imperfect blooms or dried material the past.

Thorny plants are never used because of their unpleasant connotations, and this is also true of any poisonous plant, however beautiful.

Certain flowers are considered symbolic of specific emotions and are selected for use in arrangements prepared for the greeting of an honored guest, as gifts, and to celebrate seasonal holidays.

There is also sex symbolism expressed in the flowers used, strong colors being considered as male, and blues, whites, and yellows as female. Because of the dominance of the male in Eastern civilization, perfect blooms represent the male, while immature and imperfect flowers are female. Shrubs and trees are male, while small blossoms are female. These are but a few of the many phases of sex symbolism in Japanese flower art.

In the freer and less conventional modern Japanese schools, these symbolic meanings—owing to Occidental influence and education—are less strictly adhered to.

BRIEF STUDIES OF A FEW JAPANESE STYLES

The flower artist can gain much by a study of authentic Japanese work. It is not necessary to follow slavishly the principles which govern Oriental floral art, but familiarity with these is a good basis for creating original line designs.

A number of books, illustrated by colored sketches, have been printed in Japan and are on sale in the United States. A study of these—or, better yet, of exhibitions of authentic Japanese arrangements—is well worth while. From them the arranger learns the difference between the formal or classical forms and the freer, modern interpretations of Japanese principles. Such study also familiarizes the student with the superb balance, rhythmic curves, and fine sense of design which characterizes Japanese flower art.

PLATE 43. *MINIATURES*

*The flower artist who becomes skillful at making miniatures will find al-
most daily use for them in home decoration, particularly for the breakfast
nook, mantles, and window sills; and as a charming gesture in the guest
room.*

Arrangements by members of the Federated Garden Clubs of New
   York State
International Flower Show, New York
Class: Miniature arrangements.

Classical Forms. In the strictly formal Japanese arrangement, only restrained curves are used, artificially bent branches and stems not being permitted. No leaves or blooms may touch the

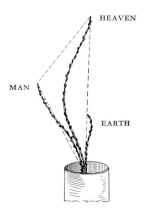

Formal Vertical Arrangement

edge of the container and horizontal lines are taboo.

Because the emphasis in classical forms is almost entirely on line, the groupings have little depth and are tall and slim. Of course the skeleton is triangular. If the apex of the triangle formed is toward the left, the arrangement is a left-hand grouping. If toward the right, a right-hand one. (See above.) The stems are closely joined for several inches above the water line, and the plant material occupies not more than one-half the opening of the container. Tall jars are used for this type of arrangement and the effect of the arrangement is one of height and slenderness.

More than three lines may be used but the added subsidiary branches always come within the main skeleton without overshadowing it. (See below.)

Seven-Line Arrangement—
The Three Chief Elements Remaining Dominant

Semi-classical. Less formal arrangements of the same general type employ freer curves, giving more breadth and depth to the composition. Artificially forced curves are used and a group of contrasting flowers (called *Nejime*) may be placed

Nejime

Flowers added at base forming "earth" element

near the place where the closely grouped main stems enter the water; not in front of the main stem line but slightly before it and to one side, "in the ideal way" as the Japanese put it. *Nejime* may be used to replace the lowest, or Man, element, c. Semi-classical groupings are placed

PLATE 44. *SIMPLICITY*

This reproduction illustrates the possibility in using just one or two kinds of flowers for simple home decorations. Here the colors of trumpet daffodils with their own foliage are repeated in the base and container.

Mrs. Charles Hoffman, Scarsdale (N. Y.) Garden Club
Judges' Course of the Federated Garden Clubs of New York State
Class: Luncheon table arrangement, one or two in form of candlesticks.

in containers especially designed for them, including the standing jars with three legs with
plate-like tops, called *usubata*. Containers for
semi-formal groupings are broader and less tall
than those selected for strictly classical arrangements.

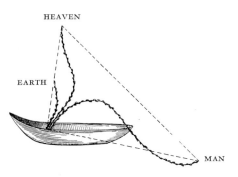

HEAVEN

EARTH

MAN

Informal Horizontal Arrangement

Informal line arrangements. A third style which
follows the same general trend in composition,
permits wide, free-curving and even horizontal
lines, and is deeper.

Hanging baskets, and boats, wall vases, and
the bamboo vases with two or more openings are
especially suited to the informal style.

Arrangements of this type placed in hanging
baskets or wall vases or suspended boats are often

composed of freely curving vines presenting a horizontal triangular form. (See page *180*.)

In the boat groupings, the plant material used represents the sails, masts, etc., and the placement is indicative of favorable winds or seasonal weather conditions. These special rules are too complicated to go into here, but the Westerner who possesses a boat container can probably attain a more distinguished composition if she thinks of the material she is using in it as indicative of the masts and sails of the little craft.

The double tier arrangements, also of the informal type, are placed in bamboo containers with side openings cut between the sections of the bamboo. These groupings have found little favor so far in this country probably because to our eyes they have an artificiality which is almost awkward.

At the top of the container above the upper bamboo joint a space holds water and the upper arrangement, which is sometimes a small triangular spray, the "Heaven" line of which extends above the topmost point of the upper arrangement, being one and one-half times the height of the entire container.

Another plan for the double tier composition is to use a smaller grouping in the lower tier—one which is one and one-half times the height of the lower solid segment; and in the upper portion, a horizontal arrangement, the longest line of which —extending horizontally—is one and one-half times the height of the entire vase.

In all arrangements which extend horizontally, the A or Heaven line, which is always vertical because it reaches toward the sky, is the one of intermediate length while the Man line, B, becomes the longest line, extending horizontally.

NAJEIRE

The most informal type of Japanese arrangement, called *Najeire*, which means "flowers stuck in a container," developed after a period of extreme formality. In recent years it has been revived in modified form.

Najeire arrangements maintain the triangular skeleton but lean at a sharp angle from the container which is usually deep and pillar-like. (See page *184.*) The stems are held in place by split twigs forced across the mouth of the vase just be-

PLATE 45. *BREATH OF SPRING*

*Daffodils and a few budded shrub branches—but note the interest added by
the way the twigs are bent, the unopened daffodil bud, and the "hand" of
rhododendron leaves; also the way the base picks up the color of the twigs.*

Mrs. Elbert A. Bach, Flushing (L. I.) Garden Club
Daffodil Show of the Horticultural Society of New York
Class: An arrangement of narcissi suitable for a hall table;
 honorable mention.

[183]

Najiere

low the surface of the water. In the modified modern forms, erect groupings also come under this heading, but are freely and informally arranged.

MORIBANA

As modern times brought more naturalistic and less stylized forms to Japanese flower art, *Moribana* arrangements came into favor. These groupings are placed in low open dishes and reproduce in miniature a scene from Nature. This type of composition is widely used by American artists.

A *Moribana* grouping may consist of a single triangular arrangement placed near one end of a shallow oblong or oval dish, with an expanse of

[184]

PLATE 46. *SPRING GOLD*

*In this delightful basket arrangement there is none of the usual stiffness
and heaviness. The few "heavy" flowers are placed low, with starry ones
and the maple twigs well above them to give an airy effect.*

Mrs. Otto H. Langhans, Flushing (L. I.) Garden Club
Daffodil Show of the Horticultural Society of New York
Class: Basket of narcissi arranged for effect; 2nd prize.

water and moss and rocks to simulate shore, islands, etc. Or it may have one large and two or more smaller flower groupings. In a three-group arrangement of this sort, triangular place-

Moribana

ment of the three arrangements is adhered to, so that if the composition is viewed from above the placement of the groups in the dish forms a tri-angle. (See figure.) Each of the groups used in a *Moribana* composition is complete in itself—a perfect triangular arrangement—and these are combined to form a larger triangle.

The flowers selected for *Moribanas*, the color of the rocks, the expanse of water, and the material used for shore, indicate the season which the artist wishes to represent and here again the rules are quite precise and rigid.

Three triangular groups of daffodils with foliage, in a long low dish, with young turf near the edge and an expanse of water visible, is indicative of spring. Or a branch of flowering cherry or plum may be arranged near one edge of a low container, overhanging the water. This depicts a living tree blooming on a low bank over a pool. The branch or branches used maintain a triangular form and near the trunk is placed a group of tiny spring flowers (*Nejime*, page *178*). Small rocks peeping from the water give an effect of islands or stepping stones and turf near the branch represents the shore.

A gnarled dwarf evergreen placed in sand or moss with little water visible in the container and with black stones and a wisp or two of dried grass would be a winter theme; while a fruited persimmon branch simulating a living tree might be combined with small-flowered chrysanthemums to typify autumn.

"One Flower" Arrangements

A "one flower" arrangement is often contrived by the Japanese artist from a blossom left over from a more pretentious composition. These *Ichi-rin-ike* can be very lovely indeed and are an

One-Flower Arrangement

example of what may be done in the way of artistic flower decoration by anyone who can come by a single fine bloom with foliage. A single camellia, gardenia, rose, peony, or even an iris or daffodil bloom can be arranged in triangular design by the employment of foliage and perhaps an aspiring bud. The one flower arrangement is ideal for times of the year when flowers are scarce and expensive.

PLATE 47. *"DAFFS" AND FORSYTHIA*

Here is material that can be found in any April garden, with a glass con-
tainer that shows the water, thus heightening the suggestion of Spring.
The horizontal forsythia spray is somewhat too long. One about a third
shorter, and tapering to a point, would have improved the design.

Mrs. Otto H. Langhans, Flushing (L. I.) Garden Club
Daffodil Show of the Horticultural Society of New York
Class: An arrangement of narcissi suitable for a hall table.

MECHANICS

In the mere mechanics of arranging flowers, the Japanese have had much to teach us. They are masters of the art of bending branches into graceful curves. This is accomplished by placing the plant material under water for a time and then gently bending with the fingers until the desired curves are obtained.

The Japanese treatment of flowers after cutting is a study in itself. Some have wine or saline solution pumped into their stems. The stems of others are burned or dipped in hot water or alcohol, wine, or vinegar. While the masters of Japanese flower art understand these treatments and swear by them, they are reluctant to divulge their secrets to the uninitiated. The burning or searing of the stems of fragile flowers is a method practiced here in the West for preservation but other Japanese treatments are practiced only by the few who have learned from a Japanese teacher.

The ingenious Oriental methods of holding flower stems in place can be helpful to all who arrange flowers.

If a flower stem is too short for an arrangement to be placed in a tall, opaque container, the stem is spliced to a straight branch or twig, the splice coming below the water line of the vase.

In order to hold stems in exact place in a straight sided container, a stout branch of soft wood (apple or willow is good) is split at one end to form a fork. The branch is cut to fit snugly across the diameter of the container, and forced in just below the water line with the stems of the arrangement clamped in the fork at the desired height and angle. Crossed, split branches, forming four spaces for stems of the arrangement can be forced across the mouth of a container in the same way. These are bound together in the center, to keep them from shifting.

Holders. The heavy metal holders with needle points and a supplementary heavy metal piece divided into sections which sets down over the needle points, are strong enough to hold stout branches of shrubs or trees. Needle point holders, smaller in size, in crescent shapes, are designed for use in the smaller groupings of a *Moribana* composition. Metal holders with larger openings and no needle points are designed for bulbous plants.

[191]

Containers. Since special styles of Japanese flower art demand containers of certain types, many beautiful vases and dishes are designed and created for arrangements of each kind. Though these are exquisite in themselves, they are never highly colored or of flamboyant design. They are intended to form a neutral but enhancing background for the flowers they hold.

Some of the types most used are:

Straight sided, pillar-like jars or vases of bamboo, wood, pottery, porcelain or metal.

Tall pottery bottles.

Tall vases with curving sides, openings small in proportion to their greatest diameter.

Two-tier straight sided containers of bamboo with side openings.

Containers with wide, flat, plate-like tops, narrow necks, bulging bodies, standing on three legs, usually of bronze, called *usubata*.

Standing vases with fish handles.

Hand-made baskets with metal water holders concealed in them.

Low, open dishes, oblong or oval, flat bottomed or supported on very short legs.

Wall vases, gourds, and baskets.

PLATE 48. *TABLE PIECE*

A pleasing group which might have been improved by placing the smaller (Poeticus) daffodils above the larger flowered ones. In Japanese flower art it would not be permissible to use the pothos foliage (from a house plant) with garden blooms; but it adds a nice touch.

Mrs. William Joy, Jamaica, Long Island
Daffodil Show of the Horticultural Society of New York
Class: Arrangement of narcissi suitable for a hall table; 2nd prize.

Hanging vases or baskets suspended on three cords or chains, often of wood, or crescent-shaped and made of pottery.

Boat-shaped containers of wood, bamboo, pottery, or porcelain either for use on tables or to be suspended from the ceiling by chains.

Stands. The stand on which the flower container is often placed is an important part of the Japanese arrangement. The position of the vase or dish on the stand helps to create perfect balance. The use of such stands has become widespread in this country, especially for exhibition work in the "big shows." (See pages *3* and *11*.)

These stands vary widely in design and material used. Some are ornate, often of carved teakwood. Others are unevenly shaped natural wooden slabs, cut from a tree trunk. Red or black laquer trays are also employed, and oval or oblong wooden or metal stands with or without legs. Little oblong "rafts" or mats made of slender bamboo sections fastened near the ends with cord are also popular. (See page *209*.)

Staging. In Japan, arrangements are placed or "staged" in the alcove built for that purpose in the room where guests are received. In addition

PLATE 49. *FROZEN LOVELINESS*

*Crisp and fresh as a mint julep is this out-of-the-ordinary daffodil arrange-
ment in which the bold crescent curve is completed under water. The container selected gives the effect—heightened by the cracked mirror used as a
base—of a cake of ice.*

Mrs. Frederick W. Lewis, Little Neck (L. I.) Garden Club
Daffodil Show of the Horticultural Society of New York
Class: An arrangement of narcissi suitable for a hall table; 1st prize.

to the arrangement this alcove contains only an incense burner, and a single picture or hanging scroll. The composition is faced right or left according to the position of the scroll and is placed so that the scroll is not obscured by the flowers.

The idea of using several arrangements about one room as we do in America is abhorrent to Oriental taste. The one arrangement, placed in the alcove is the decorative feature of the room and other groupings would be considered distracting. With this in mind it is well to select carefully the proper setting for a Japanese arrangement. An alcove or neutral wall, without any objects cluttering the space nearby is in the spirit of such a composition.

XII

Mass Arrangements

THE TRADITIONAL MASS TREATMENT of cut flowers is exemplified in the "floral pieces" of the old Flemish, French, and Dutch masters.

Classes in the spirit of these time-honored museum pieces are occasionally featured at the "big shows." Sometimes a painting is copied slavishly with living material. Or an original composition is created in the old style.

By referring to the illustration (page 57) showing a recent replica of an early mass arrangement, the reader will observe that abundance of material; rich contrasts and blendings of color; and a nice sense of balance, unity, and focus are combined to produce a most admirable and distinctive flower picture.

Though the conception and treatment are very different from that of modern floral art, the mass arrangement, when well executed, is a triumph of rich color and effective design.

Mass Dimensions

Since the laws of design apply to any and all compositions, in whatever style they may be executed, the traditional mass arrangement will be found to conform in height, which is approximately one and a half times that of the container; and in *breadth*—a more elastic dimension—which varies with the plant material used and the type of balance (symmetrical or asymmetrical). (See page *65*.) It is in *depth* (from front to back) that the mass arrangement diverges from the normal modern arrangement. In order to accommodate the profusion of material needed for a conventional mass composition, the depth must be considerable. A mass arrangement is, in fact, often as thick through as it is broad.

PLATE 50. *JUST DWARF MARIGOLDS*

In any summer garden may be found gay dwarf marigolds. Usually when cut they are jammed into a tight mass. Here most of the foliage has been removed, but notice how effectively the few remaining leaves and the one bud have been employed.

Mrs. George Loflund, Hollis (L. I.) Woman's Club
Show of the American Dahlia Society
Class: An arrangement of marigolds; 1st prize.

A large container with a broad base and generous opening is usually selected so that the flowers and foliage may appear well balanced when banked deeply and in the profusion which characterizes this type of composition.

In using a large quantity of material, the artist must exercise unusual vigilance in preserving focal interest, balance, and unity. Though a wide color range is permissible and desirable, it is necessary to bear in mind the apparently greater weight of dark colored and full-blown flowers and the fact that the many colors are most effective when placed in groups or drifts. An unpleasing spotty appearance results from mixing carelessly blooms of different colors.

VICTORIAN ARRANGEMENTS

Victorian compositions, like all things Victorian, are ornate, somewhat heavy, and robustly colorful. They constitute the Nineteenth-Century exemplification of mass treatment. Such of our grandmothers' flowers as camellias, fuchsias, roses, tulips, stocks, and pansies lend themselves to the Victorian style. Victorian containers are

PLATE 51. *AN ARMFUL OF "GLADS"*

While not meant to be an "arrangement," in the flower show sense, this simple method of arranging the spikes displays the beauty of the individual flowers, as contrasted with their usual jammed appearance in a narrow-mouthed container.

Bowl of gladiolus in tones of red, yellow, and brown.

so distinctive as to need no description here. They are the perfect vases for the company of the black walnut and red plush which are to be found in Victorian living rooms.

FRENCH ARRANGEMENTS

Arrangements in the French manner, though more airy and delicate than medieval or Victorian compositions, fall definitely in the "mass" category.

Beautiful porcelain, glass, or marble urns of classical design and soft coloring are the preferred containers, and such flowers as narcissus, lilies, lilacs, roses, freesias, iris, and delphinium are appropriate material. French arrangements attain a feathery, lacelike effect above the focal center by the liberal use of long, slim-stemmed flowers such as delphinium, freesias, or French Roman hyacinths. (See page *49*.)

Delicate or pastel color effects are another characteristic of French compositions. Yellows, mauves, pale blues, pinks, and whites are blended to produce a dainty and subdued color pattern, like the soft and delicately tinted silk upholstery

PLATE 52. *HARMONY IN RED AND GOLD*

Here again the advantage of avoiding over-crowding in arranging summer flowers (which were not available) would have added interest. The background and table cloth lend emphasis to the color harmony.

Mrs. Robert R. Kearfott, Mamaroneck (N. Y.) Garden Club
Bowl of red and gold marigolds.

on satinwood furniture of French design. (See
page *53*.)

MODERN MASS ARRANGEMENTS

Coming down to the present day, we have an
excellent exponent of modified mass composition
in the English authority, Mrs. Constance Spry.

Her art, which developed from the problems
facing her in decorating large English homes, is a
skillful blending of abundant plant material, gay
color, and unusual, often ornate and conspicuous,
containers. It is her original and extremely free
treatment of these elements which lends character
and verve to all her compositions.

Though she lays emphasis on mass effect rather
than on line or silhouette, her work shows a
modern feeling and may some day be known by
some such title as "Twentieth-Century English."

The modern American mass arrangement is more
set and conventional in form, and shows greater
restraint in the quantity of material and the colors
used, as well as in the selection of containers.
(See page *87*.) It depends for its effect on superb
color combinations and perfectly placed material.

XIII

Line Arrangements

*L*INE ARRANGEMENT, as practiced in America today, is really a happy combination of the best features of Japanese and mass flower art.

Although line and silhouette are the key features of such compositions, the bars of conventional Japanese formalism have been let down. Since the taboos of cut and dried rules are not present, the imagination of the artist has free rein. Blooms and foliage are often massed at the focal center, giving a substantial heart to the composition, while the upper and outer portions are carried in beautiful and graceful lines of stem, leaf, or flower spray. Symmetrical or asymmetrical balance is used according to the preference of the arranger. (See pages *131* and *141*.)

PLANT MATERIAL

Almost any plant material is suitable for line treatment. Even such heavy-headed beauties as peonies, roses, tulips, or lilies can be arranged to advantage. (See page *21*.) Here the Japanese influence is strongly evident because, in order to attain a graceful line design, the large full-blown flowers are grouped low at the focal point while foliage, long-stemmed closed buds, or small flowers are used for line emphasis.

Common garden flowers, too, from the spring-flowering bulbs of April and May to the hardy chrysanthemums of October, make satisfactory material for line compositions if proper restraint is exercised in the quantity of material used. (See pages *195* and *199*.)

Exotics such as gardenias, camellias, and orchids are especially satisfactory because of the perfection of individual blossoms and leaves. (See page *29*.)

PLATE 53. *BIG ZINNIAS*

*Big flowers with short stems, no buds, and little foliage always make a
difficult problem for the arranger. Here such a condition was happily
solved. The Mexican hat and the copper container repeat the rounded form
of the blooms; and background and table assist in the color scheme.*

Mrs. Karl Von Wenckstern, Blauvelt, New York
Copper pot with David Burpee zinnias.

The use of interesting foliage—dracaena, dief-fenbachia, Rex begonia, passion vine, *Cobaea scandens*, or even the leaves of the humble blood-root—are increasing in popularity as supplementary plant material for line treatment. (See pages *137* and *195*.)

CONTAINERS

In the matter of containers, as in the selection of plant material, there is a wide latitude. Almost anything from a chopping bowl to a trench helmet may be utilized, while modern glass, pottery, porcelain, metal, and wood offer a varied assortment of good neutral colors and symmetrical forms.

The use of stands of wood or metal helps to give character and distinction to many line compositions, and the backgrounds against which they are shown can make or break flower pictures. Although figured backgrounds are often effective, plain neutral colors are safest to use, and generally to be preferred. Where an arrangement is to be photographed, a plain background is almost invariably better than a figured one.

PLATE 54. *LATE SUMMER*

Large dahlias are difficult to handle in an arrangement, but here the rather massive container keeps them from appearing top-heavy. There is a subtle tie-up, too, between the cactus type of the blooms and the needle-edged holly foliage.

Mrs. Jesse B. Perlman, Ossining (N. Y.) Woman's Club
Show of the American Dahlia Society
1st prize and Tricolor.

Special Points in Making Line Arrangements

The most important considerations in constructing a line arrangement are:

1. Selection of material, the stems or branches of which assume beautifully curved or angled lines; blossoms or buds which are individually interesting; and foliage distinctive in shape, texture and, if possible, in color.

2. Selection of a container which harmonizes or contrasts well in form, color, and texture.

3. The careful placing of the main lines or skeleton in their permanent position.

4. Development of a central point of interest—probably with a group of flowers and some foliage.

5. Intelligent pruning of confusing and unnecessary twigs, leaves, and flowers to give further emphasis to lines and silhouettes of individual blooms, buds, and leaves.

XIV

Modern Arrangements

*I*T IS QUITE NATURAL that present day trends in art should be reflected in cut flower compositions. A room furnished in the modern manner requires special floral groupings in the same spirit.

Modern arrangements, like modern paintings, sculpture, or fabrics may be of sure, bold design, striking in their originality, and recognized by most observers as sounding an important new note of beauty; or they may be so revolutionary in conception and execution that only a comparatively small cult of "educated" minds find them understandable or pleasing.

The arrangements reproduced on pages *105* and *131* are in the former class. The few large colorful elements employed in the former to present a flower design symmetrically balanced give an impression of bold sureness in both form and color. Though clivia is one of the most ungraceful and difficult of flowers because of its heavy head and nude, stiff stalk, in this instance its burning color and fine form have been most effectively handled.

In the arrangement on page *109* the artist has depended largely on form and line for her effect, attaining a distinctive and impressive design despite the subdued color key of the scheme.

The more radical and less easily understood school of modern arrangement is illustrated by such compositions as the six imitations of Dali shown by the Federated Garden Clubs of New York at the 1940 International Show and by the arrangement that won the Fenwick Medal of the Garden Club of America in the previous year.

In a modern composition, such as the one reproduced on page *131*, the geometric angularity of the design which is carried out in both material and container is reminiscent of cubism in the world of art, or of the "abstractions" which are

[212]

viewed with respectful admiration by many art lovers. In this particular instance the strong color contrasts and clean-cut, symmetrical design are striking enough to impress even the un-initiated.

Bold horizontal lines forming the broad base of a triangular design, derived from Japanese floral art, are often used in modern groupings. These compositions have a somewhat blowsy appear-ance because the long stems extending far beyond the rim of the container, almost at right angles to the vertical, seem to have fallen from place into a comfortable reclining position. They are satisfactory, however, especially for modern table decoration in that they extend the base of the arrangement without making it heavy or mas-sive. They have a theatrical boldness which is in the spirit of modern decoration and possess the virtue of seeming less formal and self-conscious than most modern arrangements.

Typically modern plant material such as strelitzias, anthuriums, calla lilies, and san-sevieria, pandanus, or other lance-like foliage, lend themselves admirably to the glorification of line and silhouette in modern arrangements.

Every year additional blooms and leaves are "discovered" and utilized for distinctive effects.

A few years ago modern arrangements were frequently shown in angular or box-like containers of neutral pottery or glass. Today ornate or richly colorful vases are often preferred. (See page *105*.) The symmetrical forms and exquisite texture of Scandinavian glass and china or pottery are equally popular. In short, it is no longer the container which sets the pace for a modern arrangement. Most containers and many plant materials can be treated in the modern manner.

XV

Miniatures

THE ART of arranging very small flowers in diminutive containers requires careful selection of material, a good sense of design, and special attention to scale.

Most of the big flower shows include classes in Miniature Arrangement and there is a place for them in the home on dressing tables or other small tables, in rooms of limited space, etc.

In show classes, the outside dimensions of the arrangement are given (usually four to six inches over-all) and the contestant is required to keep her composition within these space limits. A study of show prize-winners will prove helpful to the amateur who wishes to make miniature arrangements for the home.

A rather special talent is needed for successfully creating miniatures. The artist must have an eye for detail; must be able to "see" the tiny blooms which many of us trample under foot without notice; must have deft and skillful fingers, and a nice sense of proportion.

Containers

Antique shops and modern stores alike offer a wide selection in miniature containers. Scandinavian and Holland Glass, Royal Copenhagen ware, rare old American glass, precious French chinas, Oriental porcelain—all these sources and many more may be tapped for the very small but distinctive flower container. Arrangers whose pocketbooks prevent them from acquiring a large collection of high quality, full-size containers can indulge their love of beauty by collecting rhythmically shaped and subtly colored miniature vases, bowls, and dishes. Tiny accessories of china, glass, pottery, or bronze can often be used.

PLATE 55. *AUTUMN*

Hardy chrysanthemums and ripe fruits are combined in this colorful autumn arrangement to which the use of an old gourd shell for the container gives a delightfully original touch.

Miss Mildred Sawyer, Associate Member of the Federated Garden
  Clubs of New York State
Fall Show of the Horticultural Society of New York
Class: Still life with autumn flowers and fruits; 2nd prize.

Another convenient feature of miniature containers is the small space they occupy. Those who live in urban apartments or small homes can house a number of such containers and accessories on a single shelf.

Such objects as a thimble, a tiny conch or snail shell, the cap of an acorn, or the shell of an English walnut can be converted into interesting miniature containers.

Plant Material

In creating a miniature arrangement, the use of very small blooms and fine foliage is essential to success. In a grouping of tiny scale, a full-blown abelia or myosotis blossom may become the focal point. The florets of such flowers as orange milkweed, spirea, lantana, verbena, and ageratum can be used singly or cut into tiny sprays which do the same work in a miniature arrangement as that performed by a spray of delphinium, stock, or Canterbury bells in a full-sized composition.

In miniatures on a somewhat larger scale, the "large" blooms creating focal interest near the center of the arrangement may be such blossoms

PLATE 56. *AUTUMN TINTS*

Here a low, broad based container has been used to give stability to a bouquet for an autumn porch table. Buckshot or sand in the container lessens the chance of accidents where winds or drafts are encountered, as on a porch, an outdoor table, or near a window.

Double Korean chrysanthemums "Lavender Lady" with foliage of Japanese maple.

as sweetheart roses, bachelor's buttons, phlox florets, violas, English daisies, harebells, crown-of-thorn blossoms, or those of the semperflorens begonia. The new type of miniature or "Tom Thumb" rose is particularly useful in small arrangements.

For miniature line arrangements, accent lines can be attained by the use of pine needles, blades of grass, crocus foliage, or fronds of rabbits' foot fern, or by employing tiny sprays of small-floreted flowers.

Wild flowers such as anemones, violets, fringed polygala, saxifrage, fringed orchises, spring beauties, or the florets of lobelia (especially cardinal flower) or mertensia lend themselves to miniature treatment. Chickweed blooms make perfect "daisies."

An eye trained to look for tiny blooms will find a wealth of miniature material on every hand.

Plants for Living Miniatures

Miniature tray gardens or terrariums survive for weeks, or even months, and can be real works of art. Arbutus blossoms or the dainty pixie moss blooms may be combined with the "British soldiers" which appear in spring on lichen growing about rotting stumps. Star and other mosses may be used with these, while height is attained by the introduction of a seedling evergreen. While these living miniatures are appreciated by grown-ups and children alike, youngsters seem to get a special thrill from creating and caring for them.

IMPORTANCE OF SCALE

The amateur who attempts a miniature arrangement often fails to observe the laws of scale. One large blossom or a few out-size leaves will throw the whole composition out. All material used should be of a size to suit the container. A well constructed miniature arrangement should look like a full-sized grouping viewed through the wrong end of a telescope. The laws of design —composition, focus, balance, and unity—hold true in the miniature as in other arrangements.

If accessories are used, care must be taken that these are small enough not to dwarf the container and flowers themselves.

CHILDREN'S MINIATURES

For some reason, children often show a special aptitude for miniature composition. To encourage this inclination gives the child excellent training for more ambitious and larger arrangements later on.

Little girls enjoy making tiny groupings of flowers for the tables of their doll houses, to place on the doll's tea table, and to decorate the small tables on which many youngsters have their own meals served.

It is easy to show the child who evinces an interest in miniature arrangement, how to construct them of the smaller flowers and how to observe the laws of design.

XVI

Table Arrangements

THE MODERN TABLE IS INCOMPLETE without some sort of decoration, usually of flowers or fruit. No longer is a floral "centerpiece" considered necessary only at a dinner party. In this decade we are all flower-conscious and want the gaiety of fresh flowers with us at mealtimes.

A Few General Rules for Table Arrangements

There are two important laws governing table arrangements. Both are strictly practical, and very easily remembered:

1. Table arrangements must be so constructed that they are equally interesting from all sides. This does not mean that each person at the table must see the same thing. Many Japanese line arrangements make splendid table pieces. But all sides of the design must be interesting and suitably arranged for observation.

2. Table arrangements must be low enough not to obstruct a diner's view of his opposite neighbor. Sometimes, at large or formal dinners where greater height is desired in the floral decorations, the vases are placed at points *between*—not opposite—the guests. This is only permissible, however, at a dinner where there is to be little or no general conversation as such a composition does obstruct one's view of his neighbor diagonally across the table.

There is wide scope for creative imagination in table decorations, and new and interesting things are constantly being done in this field. As a general rule, simplicity and naturalness is the desirable keynote, though some "modern" containers are made to be used in bizarre and artificial ways. However a highly complicated arrangement will usually be out of keeping.

[224]

PLATE 57. *COLOR SELECTION*

It is often the more subtle color harmonies that lend out-of-the-ordinary quality to an arrangement. Here the obvious accent on yellow in the container and the centers of the "mums" is supplemented by the green and pink color harmonies of foliage and base cloth, shrub stems and flower petals.

Fall Show of the Horticultural Society of New York
Class: Still life with autumn flowers.

MODERN TABLE ARRANGEMENTS

For instance, a low glass container, round, oblong, or oval in shape is constructed with an open center and a narrow space to hold water—rather like a canal—about the edge. These holders are planned for use with short-stemmed blossoms and are often seen packed with gardenias, camelias, the heads of carnations, or other showy blooms. Foliage is either dispensed with entirely or used in a conventional pattern.

Arrangements of this type have the virtues of being very colorful and well below the eye level of the diners, but they are so artificial as to suggest a petit point pattern or a design for cross stitch rather than a dish of living flowers.

An effect much more natural and quite as striking can be attained by placing one, two, or three showy blooms (gardenias, camellias, water-lilies, or single peonies) on the surface of the water in a very low dish of heavy modern glass or pottery. The foliage accompanying such an arrangement is used with restraint.

Low glass containers made of adjustable silver wire with small test-tube-like vases attached are sometimes used to make an unusual and colorful modern table piece, but here, even more than in the first type of container described, the result is sure to be artificial. Such holders give a feeling of fussiness and remind the sophisticated of the the bride's "shower" bouquet.

A distinctly modern effect can be reached by the use of a pineapple top with its interestingly curved lines. Purple and green alligator pears, dark plums with the bloom on them, and a green gage or two to give contrast, or a handful of polished chestnuts and a bunch of white grapes could be used with the pineapple top. Italian or other colorful pottery, or a metal or wooden tray are appropriate containers for such a motif.

The Breakfast Table

A pottery jug or pitcher, a small bean pot, or a pewter mug may be used to hold the gay and easily arranged nosegays which are appropriate on the breakfast table. Common garden flowers are the best subjects.

The color scheme is, of course, determined by the china and napery, as it must be in all table arrangements. The wise woman who selects everyday china of a pastel or neutral hue can constantly vary her table color scheme by the use of different colored linen and flowers. The soft brown or buff earthenware now so popular offers endless opportunities for color changes, as does natural wood, pewter, and softly colored pastel pottery or china in powder blue, ashes of roses, gray-green, or off-white.

A breakfast bouquet in the average home should seem to be arranged without effort—just stuck in the container. Of course the result may look less studied than it really is, but the effect should be carefree and cheerful.

Nasturtiums, coreopsis, painted daisies, calendulas, bachelors' buttons, gaillardias, climbing roses, chrysanthemums, and asters are the sort of flowers which look well on the breakfast table. In spring the minor bulbs, early flowering tulips, or small daffodils give a promise of more bloom to come. For a winter breakfast table, a small blooming houseplant in an interesting container or a spray or two of ivy may be used.

An arrangement of ripe fruit is a practical centerpiece for a breakfast party where many

PLATE 58.   *ACCENT ON FORM*

*The importance of "form emphasis" is well illustrated in this winter
monochrome of dried material that most beginners in the art of arrangement
would have passed over as not worth considering.*

Mrs. John R. Delafield, Millbrook (N. Y.) Garden Club
Arrangement of dried material in a wooden bowl.

guests are present. The contents of the tray may be devoured at the end of the meal.

LUNCHEON TABLES

Whether the luncheon be a family affair or a "party," flowers are needed. Colorful linen or the natural linen scarves and cloths which are so beautifully decorated with peasant drawn work or cross stitch help set the stage for the table arrangement. By picking up one or two of the colors in the linen, the hostess may make an arrangement which is a melodious accompaniment to her table and its setting.

Some hostesses plan the table arrangement to match or enhance their own costumes or those of their guests of honor. Others create compositions which set the theme for the gathering. Just as robust, strongly-colored flowers are used to decorate the table or buffet at a hunt breakfast, so the woman who is lunching a romantic poet who is later to speak at her club, may create a classical atmosphere by decorating her table with freesias, lilies, or orchids. Nature lovers will enjoy a living tray garden; and if the guest

XVII

The Present Trend

$\mathcal{T}$HE PRESENT TREND HERE in America is, on the whole, a healthy one. Common sense is reasserting itself. If any criticism is to be made, the tendency toward too many conventionalized designs may be objected to. Since American women are so passionately absorbed in the art, and since their rivalry is so keen, there is a temptation to employ an academic formalism which they know the all-powerful judges will recognize and accept. Because of this trend, the radical modernists introduce a stimulating divergence from the accepted standard, as does such carefree work as that done by Mrs. Constance Spry.

After the close study of recent accomplishment in the field of flower arrangement made by the authors in the preparation of this book, it is evident to them that each new season brings a higher standard in selection of plant material, containers, accessories, and backgrounds, and in the designs created with these elements.

Modified line compositions are the rule— proved by a few notable exceptions. (See pages *25* and *29*.) The lines of the taller stems and branches, and the silhouettes of individual flowers and leaves are made to count quite as strongly as the groupings of flowers and foliage at the focal center. (See page *45*.) The best features of mass and line composition are thus combined. As "arrangers" cast about constantly for new plant material and containers, the range of color, form, and texture increases with every show.

On the other hand, those whose interest in arrangement is simply to provide beauty in the home, are busily experimenting with new treatments for easily available garden-grown flowers

PLATE 61.   *FRUIT AND FOLIAGE*

*Another example of the possibilities inherent in arrangements made with
a single kind of flower or other material—in this instance kumquat foliage
and fruit. The use of just the right background adds materially.*

Mrs. Frederick W. Lewis, Little Neck (L. I.) Garden Club
International Flower Show, New York
Class: Pedestal arrangement of tropical foliage, fruit on branches
   or stems permitted, tall container required; 2nd prize.

and foliage plants. All the best compositions are not seen at the "big shows." Many an exquisite flower picture is created for and enjoyed only by the immediate family of the artist. This is as it should be, for, although thousands of interested spectators may view a prize winner at a flower show, the pleasure derived at home from a beautiful arrangement is more intimate and probably more inspirational to those for whom it is executed.